COMES THE
MILLENNIUM

ST. MARTIN'S PRESS
NEW YORK

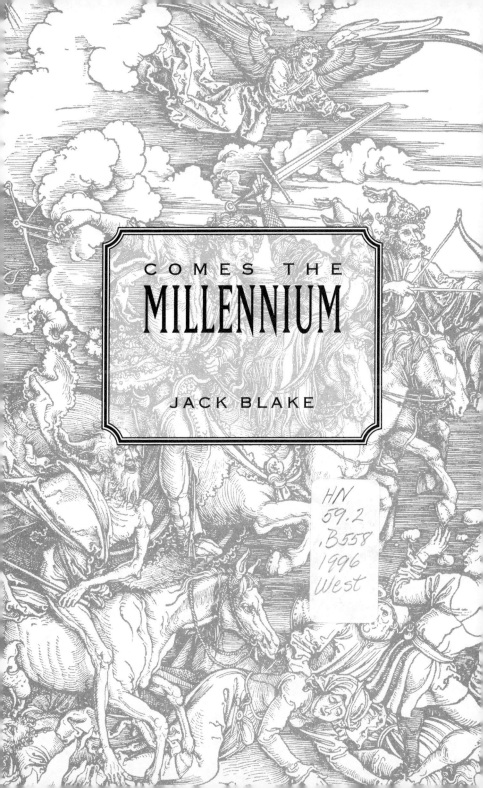

COMES THE
MILLENNIUM

JACK BLAKE

PUBLISHED BY THOMAS DUNNE BOOKS
An imprint of St. Martin's Press

Design by Nancy Resnick

ISBN 0-312-14571-3

First edition: October 1996

10 9 8 7 6 5 4 3 2 1

A grand transcendental fiction is to be understood as an irrational but compelling blend of the religious impulse to seek salvation, of the nationalistic self-identification as being superior to outsiders, and of utopian social doctrines reduced to the level of populist slogans. Permitting escape from unsatisfactory reality through a commitment to an imaginary reality yet to be achieved, metamyth served to galvanize and channel mass passions . . .

—Zbigniew Brzezinski, in *Out of Control*, beginning his discussion of the massive death and brutality brought about by Hitler, Stalin, and Mao

CONTENTS

PART I
BASIC PRINCIPLES

ONE

RATIONAL PEOPLE

If you are a rational person, this book is for you. If you are not a rational person, then put this book back where you found it. Why? Because *Comes the Millennium* may make you furious. Nobody needs that kind of stress in his or her life. Besides, the last televangelist I watched said the world is going to end in rapture before very long anyway, so there'll be no need for this book. But rational people should hang on to it just in case the guy was wrong.

The world is in a mess. On the other hand, some part of the world has always been in a mess. During the period from the collapse of the Roman Empire to the Renaissance, for example, the life of an average human being, at least in Europe, was hellish. If we had to live like people lived during the Dark Ages, then we'd think the world had already come to an end. If life as a serf seemed intolerable, then a person could join a Crusade and get a real taste of slaughter, rape, pillage, plunder, starvation, failure, and multiculturalism. Nowadays, parochial school athletic teams take up nicknames like "the Crusaders."

Humans do a number of things beautifully, but primarily these are the individual productions such as art, music, literature, and acts of altruistic heroism. Humans also do a number of things in ugly, brutal, and self-destructive fashion, and often these are collective productions such as the Spanish Inquisition and the Joseph McCarthy hearings. There is a simple rule that separates the beautiful individual productions from the ugly collective ones, namely: *If given enough power, any organized system of beliefs, from Western religion to totalitarian political regimes, will behave in a way that guarantees a full measure of human misery.* That misery then will be presented as evidence that the human race, or some segment of it, is evil and must be destroyed.

Then a prophet may come forth to predict the final battle between good and evil, the salvation of believers, the destruction of nonbelievers, and the end of the world or a utopian state. The day all this happens could be tomorrow, but December 31, 1999, has a certain allure, largely because of the use of the term *millennium* in Christian literature. If we fall prey to that allure, then our behavior is likely to change for the crazier the closer we get to December 31, 1999. That's why I wrote this book; it's my attempt to reduce the influence of the crazies.

Rational people are individual human beings who see no obvious reason for letting the world collapse into chaos, violence, misery, and despair and at the same time wonder whether some of the right kind of human efforts might forestall what their favorite televangelist is calling the Rapture but what looks suspiciously like plain old ethnic cleansing, AIDS, nuclear irresponsibility, and global ecological disaster. Rational people likely also wonder if indeed all the human misery they see, read about, and maybe experience is truly foreordained or maybe whether that misery is something that humanity has brought upon itself by being irrational when it needed to be objective, patient, understanding, mutually respectful, and well educated. So I wrote this book for those who believe a responsible citizen shouldn't just stand by and watch the world go to hell and who believe they have the power, even as individuals, to do something about it.

Rational people exhibit a number of characteristic behaviors:

they read the newspaper, including the comics, editorials, letters, and classified; watch cable news telecasts, including the boring Senate and House committee hearings; read nonfiction books with relatively few pictures; read newsmagazines; talk about local, national, and international political issues; ask intelligent questions; and care about their children. Rational people work hard and generally obey the law, letting others live their own lives unless those other lives have some kind of negative impact on associated individuals or society as a whole.

Rational people pray wherever and whenever they damn well please, if they please, to whatever god, gods, or goddesses they damn well please to pray to. Rational people respect the rights of others, including irrational people, to pray to whomever and whatever they, too, wish to pray to, including 1964 Ford station wagons, the birdbath, a fuzzy caterpillar, or a rattlesnake. Rational people know that they have never been harmed by someone else's praying to a 1964 Ford station wagon. Rational people also know that they have a perfect right and privilege to go to one of America's main line churches, participate honestly in the service, listen to an intelligent, uplifting sermon that relies on the Bible as metaphor, then go back home feeling even more human and rational than when they left for church earlier that morning. Even rational people who consider themselves atheists usually appreciate a well-done sermon that addresses current issues of good and evil in an intelligent, literary, and insightful way.

In short, rational people think for themselves, encourage others to do the same, and evaluate the world's events in a reasonably objective manner based on knowledge instead of desires. Rational people try very hard to see the world for what it really is, rather than what they *believe* it to be. Rational people don't always succeed in their efforts. It's not easy to be rational. Human beings are very easily duped, hypnotized, herded into submission, convinced that the truth right before their eyes is in fact a lie, or that a bald-faced lie is the honest-to-God truth.

There are many examples of such collective stupidity in any decent library; the quickest way to find one is to look up "Nazi Germany" in the card catalog.

The overriding trait of rational people is that they do not confuse their own opinions and desires with correct solutions to social and political problems. Of course, one's own opinions and desires *might* coincide with the correct solutions to these problems, but a perfect match is just a coincidence. Rational people are especially skeptical of assertions presented as facts, then used, as if they were facts, to justify attitudes and decisions about any matter of public interest. This transparent political tactic has been used to support positions on health care costs, taxes, entitlements, the environment, public school curricula, violent crime, abortion, sexual orientation, and military intervention in a vicious holy war, to name just a few of the issues that seem to be tearing away at our national fabric. A rational person knows that assertions need to be tested in some way before their validity can be determined and that majority opinion is not a valid test of any assertion.

In a surprising number of cases, politically charged assertions have already been tested and the information needed to determine whether they are true is easily accessible. Anyone who's pressed for time can stop by the library, look up our old friend Nazi Germany, and quickly find an example of a tested assertion, namely: Germany will be better off without the Jews. Substitute any nation for "Germany" and any category of human being in the place of "Jews" and you will have an assertion some presently living despot and/or elected official claims is a fact. United States Senator Jesse Helms, for example, believes that the United States would be better off without homosexuals in its population. So did the Nazis. In fact, the Nazis *would* have been much better off without homosexuals in the *British* population. Alan Turing, the famous British homosexual and mathematical genius, broke the Germans' codes during World War II and in doing so came close to single-handedly ensuring the success of the Normandy invasion. In all his pious ranting about homosexuals, Jesse Helms never mentions Alan Turing.

Rational people try not to confuse anecdotal information with statistical information. That is, they do not extend their personal experience to society as a whole. Why not? Because society, especially American society, is a highly diverse and complex phenomenon, not a simple and homogeneous one. If American society were simple and homogeneous, then it is likely anyone's personal experience would be illustrative of conditions in society as a whole. But our society is neither simple nor homogeneous. Instead, it is *very* complex and heterogeneous.

Certain political leaders have the power, however, to make a large number of people think that American society is simple and homogeneous. Ronald Reagan had more of this kind of power than almost any other postwar elected leader. Reagan had the body language to convince the American public to believe almost anything. He performed this function so well as president that I wonder why he never won an Academy Award as an actor. Reagan's failure as an actor probably tells us more about the American presidency than about Reagan. The American presidency gives a person power that real actors have to earn with their talents. Thus Reagan, a truly mediocre actor, ended up with an enormous amount of power to convince irrational people that personal anecdote was reflective of society as a whole. People like Dustin Hoffman and Robert De Niro, however, are truly great actors who earn their power and rarely try to convince the American public that their personal anecdote should be the basis for our national foreign policy. Had Ronald Reagan been equal to the power that befell him, the world would be a much better place than it is today. For example, Reagan had the body language to slow down population growth, ease racial tensions, and reduce environmental destruction. Instead, he chose to use his mediocre acting skills suddenly blessed with enormous power to make these problems worse.

Rational people are also able to determine when symbolism feeds a political agenda. Take, for example, the matter of flag burning. Burning of the American flag *in fact* is a relatively inconsequential, highly localized, and infrequent event that, if ignored, tends to go away. But the sight of someone burning an American flag infuriates many citizens, especially those who have served in the military. I am neither advocating nor condoning flag burning. In truth, I would never burn an American flag; I have a fair amount of disdain for people who burn American flags, primarily because such burning demonstrates that these people have been ineffective at accomplishing their personal agendas in any other way. If there is anything American society offers, it's a lot of ways to advance personal agendas effectively through the system. Thus flag burning is a sure sign of incompetence. That's why it will go away if ignored.

The trouble with flag burning is that a lot of irrational people refuse to ignore it. Mostly, these people are insecure, ultrareligious, ultraconservative, or ultramilitary, and sometimes dangerous combinations of all three. Although flag burners are inconsequential incompetents, United States senators who introduce constitutional amendments to make flag burning an unconstitutional act punishable as a felony are nonanalytical demagogues with true power. They should be ashamed of themselves. Today, every politician who wants it gets hours of television time (e.g., on C-Span). All he or she has to do is get on some committee that holds hearings, and committee assignment is what being in Congress is all about. Politicians get so much time, in fact, that we see how boring, prejudiced, inarticulate, and posturing they can be when given a national audience. Periodically the camera pans the "audience," and we discover mostly empty seats. Politicians, including United States senators, could establish themselves as intelligent, articulate, deepthinking, rational role models just by using the right 100 or 200 words, on national television, in response to inconsequential acts by incompetents (e.g., flag burners). One gets the impression that at least some of the senators would rather be demagogues.

What we have here is a real challenge for rational people: find out a way to make it more fun, or at least more satisfying, to be an intelligent, articulate, deep-thinking, rational role model than a demagogue. Maybe we should start by issuing each person elected to public office a historical reminder: intelligent, articulate statespersons are usually remembered; demagogues are usually ridiculed, eventually. In fact, most of them already are ridiculed.

In the following chapters, I discuss some religious and moral issues that seem to be ripping at the fabric of American life. One would hope that discussion to be fairly objective, although some will view it as outright liberal, atheistic, and decidedly humanistic. I'll admit to the last. To me, a "humanist" is a person who has compassion for his or her fellow human being; is willing to try to understand the other's feelings, circumstances, and beliefs; and places a reasonable amount of faith in humanity's ability to solve its earthly problems. *Humanist*, to me, is an uplifting, flattering, complimentary term. We should all be humanists. I don't claim to be a Biblical scholar, but I've looked pretty hard for evidence that compassion, understanding, and a willingness to work toward the common good are un-Christian attributes; there is no such evidence in the Bible.

In case anyone's wondering about my other traits, I am a little bit of a tree hugger, but I'm not a communist or a socialist or a one-worlder, and I tend to vote Republican when the Republicans put up a good candidate. I voted for Richard Nixon in my first presidential election, and would probably vote for him again if given the chance. I'm revealing all this personal political history and attitude just so readers won't think I'm a subversive communist or worse. Speaking of being thought of as worse than a communist, I'm not a homosexual, either. I don't want anyone to have the option of dismissing everything in this book just because he or she suspects it was written by a pinko-commie-fag. It wasn't. I'm happily married, and have been for 34 years, to a lovely rational woman, and I am not the least bit physically attracted to members of my own gender. We belong to, and attend (but not every Sunday), one of America's mainline churches. We have three lovely rational children. I am embarrassed to say that at least two of them are registered Democrats, but that doesn't mean they can't be rational, too, regardless of what some of my irrational acquaintances think.

A lot of our friends think I'm quirky, however, because when we're at social gatherings, I tend to talk big talk—like the stuff in this book—instead of small talk. These friends would rather talk about babies, children, small amounts of money, sports, their lawns, their parents, and their operations than about the ideas, assertions, and information in this book. These are very well educated, professional, and often financially successful people who duck the major issues of our time and waste their lives on small talk. We have a few friends, however, who talk about art, politics, big money, good books, ideas, wine, and classical music. These few sets of friends don't think I'm quirky; they are more rational than I am and are probably working on books like this one right now.

Thanks for sticking with me this far into the first chapter. Feel free to loan this book to anyone with the proviso that you get it back. People who borrow books but get told to be sure and return them think the books are important. This book also makes a great Christmas or birthday gift, say, to ultraconservative relatives who already have everything else (which is what I intend to do with my free copies). In fact, one of the reasons I wrote it is for my ultraconservative relatives. I'm sick of getting I-told-you-so types of newspaper clippings and jokes from ultraconservative relatives. And I've never listened to Rush Limbaugh, either. Well, that's not entirely true. I was driving alone through the country one night and my tape player was broken, so I had to listen to local radio stations. I accidently found Rush Limbaugh. Who is this jerk? I kept asking myself. Eventually my curiosity was satisfied, my question answered, and I turned him off.

TWO

DAYS OF RECKONING

December 31, 1999, has all the media-hype traits to be considered *the* Day of Reckoning. To the solar system, however, December 31, 1999, is just another day, and I hope it will be just another day for you, too. But the closer we get to that day, the more we will hear from fundamentalist and literalist Christians that the Lord is coming. Needless to say, I've not checked my calendar to see what day of the week the end of the millennium falls on. I hope it's on a Monday. If the end of the millennium falls on a Monday, then maybe there won't be quite so much heavy drinking and driving as there would be if it fell on, say, Friday or Saturday.

JUDGMENT DAY

Throughout Western Christian theology, one finds the concept of "judgment day." In 2 Esdras (Ezra), for example, one of the books of the Protestant Apocrypha, the archangel Uriel informs the prophet and scribe Ezra that the humanity's Heaven-on-Earth will be realized only after a time of maximum evil, that the beginning of this heavenly state will coincide with the arrival of the Messiah, after the Second Coming, and that Heaven-on-Earth will last for four hundred years. Modern televangelists routinely tell us that we are now living in the time of maximum evil, exemplified, no doubt, by rock lyrics, Roe vs. Wade, and President William Clinton's appointment of an admitted lesbian to a relatively high government post. Evidently, four hundred years was not long enough for the Christian writers and translators who added material to the beginning and end of Ezra and who increased the four hundred to a thousand. Presumably it's well within anyone's power to rewrite the Bible, as various other people did between about 722 B.C. and the 4th century A.D. (and as certain groups are trying to do now), and increase the length of the heavenly state still further. The only thing standing in the way is Revelation's admonition to neither subtract nor add to the Bible, a warning that was largely ignored for the millennium of the Bible's writing and is ignored today by various revisionist, gender-neutral scribes, and in fact, if not in writing, by those who interpret the Bible in ways that enhance their own political power.

In Revelation, the "day of reckoning" is a long, fantastic, convoluted event that ends with the battle at Armageddon, in which good triumphs over evil. With victory, an angel ties up Satan, and thus begins the millennium of heavenly bliss, wherein all the believers become priests. But the devil is only bound for a thousand years, after which time he's freed from his prison and another great battle between good and evil occurs. At the end of this battle, the earthly world ends, everyone faces God himself, and the heavenly eternity begins. A new heaven and a new Earth are made. The new holy city of the new Earth looks suspiciously like Jerusalem. The remarkably Jerusalem-like new holy city has twelve gates, each with a name of one of the twelve tribes of Israel written on it. The twelve apostle names are relegated to the footings of the city's wall. All of this is supposed to happen "shortly." "Shortly" turned out to be something more than 1900 years, the period between the writing of Revelation and 1995, and there's no real evidence that we've finished waiting for Satan to be defeated and imprisoned and the thousand (= 400) years of bliss to begin.

THE FIRST MILLENNIUM

The word *millennium* means a thousand years, but it doesn't necessarily mean the calendar date 1000 or 2000. Those dates, like the ends of decades and centuries, are strictly human constructions to help humans organize time, although admittedly the days and years do have a connection to natural cycles, namely the rotation of the Earth and the length of the Earth's orbit around the sun. In the Dark Ages (the thousand years during which the Catholic Church completely controlled Western civilization), anyone who claimed that a millennium was a multiple of Earth's rotation and/or orbit around the sun would likely have been burned at the stake. It would be interesting to determine how many of today's fundamentalist Christians believe the sun orbits a flat earth. Here is a hypothesis we can test using standard survey methods developed for political polls: The number of fundamentalist Christians who believe the Earth is flat equals the number who believe the Earth was created in 4004 B.C. Although those numbers may not be equal, I promise that neither one is zero.

Revelation was written circa A.D. 95 by a "John" who was evidently living on, and perhaps banished to, the Aegean island of Patmos. Thus 1095 was the first millennium. What was the world like in 1095? Rather miserable, of course, given the fact that 1095 was in the heyday of the Dark Ages. Satan walked the earth continually on the make, often successfully impregnating numerous women and/or using them as bait to attract men. It's not easy to determine whether Satan really was alive and stalking women or whether his presence on Earth, as well as his view of females as legitimate victims and allies, was a product of the male-dominated Church. St. Thomas Aquinas considered women less than slaves and declared that children should love their father more than their mother. Although not necessarily the first case in which Church declarations were in direct violation of basic biological principles, it was one of the most naive and elementary misconceptions of the power of religion over nature. Laws generally allowed wife beating, and if convicted of a crime against a woman, you'd be fined only half as much as if you'd committed the same crime against a man. Organized religion has always had a problem with women.

Obviously the world did not end in 1000, or in 1095, nor did the heavenly kingdom begin. In fact, the first millennium saw organized religion sink to one of its lowest states. Otto I became emperor of Germany in 962, crowned by Pope John XII. John XII made Jimmy Swaggart and Jim Bakker look pretty good by comparison. According to his cardinals, John XII had committed incest with his father's widow (= mother?), incest with his father's widow's niece, adultery with his father's concubine, and turned the Vatican into a whorehouse. There followed a quarter century of surrealism in the heartland of Christianity. Otto deposed John XII and replaced him with Leo VIII. When Otto left Rome, John grabbed the papacy again, but he died in 964 and was replaced by Benedict V, who was removed, again by Otto, who restored Leo. After Leo died, Benedict VI was strangled by a local noble who ran off to Constantinople, returning, eventually, to kill another Pope, namely John XIV. By this time, the Ottos had succeeded one another, so that Otto III came back to Rome to clean up the mess, making his own chaplain Pope Gregory V. Once Otto III had gone back to Germany, Roman Republic consul Crescentius deposed Gregory. Gregory excommunicated Crescentius and Crescentius responded by engineering the election of John XVI as pope. Otto came back to Rome, gouged out John's eyes, beheaded Crescentius, and restored Gregory, who was (probably) poisoned in 999.

I've shortened and sanitized this story from the more detailed description of it in Volume IV (The Age of Faith) of the Durants' *The Story of Civilization*. The Durants' multivolume set by that name was, and probably still is, readily available from the Book of the Month Club as a sign-up bonus or cheap dividend purchase. I couldn't find a historical record of the end of the world and the beginning of the heavenly kingdom in any of the Durant volumes or, for that matter, in any of the other publications I consulted in writing this book.

RECENT JUDGMENT DAYS

In the history of organized religion, a great many days of reckoning have been predicted. Needless to say, the vast majority of them have resulted in neither the Millennium, the Second Coming of Christ, nor in the end of the world as we know it. In a few cases, however, for a few deeply religious people, the world as they knew it did end on schedule. One of these cases occurred on November 18, 1978, when a fairly effective religious leader named Jim Jones convinced 911 of his followers it was time to die and gave them fruit punch laced with cyanide. We don't know whether either those 911 men, women, and children or the five Americans shot to death in the People's Temple's Jonestown, Guyana, enclave met Christ before they died. Nothing has happened since to convince anyone, least of all the televangelists, that Satan has been bound for his thousand years as a result of the Jonestown massacre.

In a more recent and extensively reported case, approximately seventy members of a religious cult, the Branch Davidians, burned to death in a fire on April 19, 1993, in Waco, Texas, convinced all the while they were the chosen people of God and the end of the world was coming. The media reported that when the bodies were examined after the "end of the world," some were found out to have been shot in the head. I do not know personally for a fact that these reported shootings actually occurred. The thousand years of heavenly bliss did not begin with the explosions and fires that wracked the Branch Davidian headquarters, either, although the tabloids formalized the joke that was on many people's minds—that cult leader David Koresh had escaped via a tunnel and would reappear as the resurrected Christ. And, as anyone could predict in a pre-Millennium age, a made-for-television movie about Mr. Koresh was whipped out almost before his ashes had cooled.

Both the Jonestown and Waco days of reckoning were, of course, brought about by human gullibility and not (insofar as we know) by God. In modern times, World War I comes much closer to being an enactment of Revelation than either the Jonestown or Waco debacles. The Four Horsemen of the Apocalypse appeared on schedule: a variety of fearsome foreign invaders, depending on your viewpoint *(behold a white horse: and he that sat upon him had a bow; and a crown . . . and he went forth conquering)*; war enough for all *(there went out another horse that was red: and power was given to him that sat thereon to take peace from the earth)*; postwar starvation in Germany and Russia, especially of women and children who are the victims of all wars *(lo a black horse; and he that sat on him had a pair of balances in his hand . . . A measure of wheat for a penny)*; and death—by pestilence, as in the influenza pandemic of 1918 *(behold a pale horse: and his name that sat on him was Death)*.

This vision of WWI as a model end of the world comes from Isaac Asimov's *Guide to the Bible*; others may have made the connection, too, but Asimov does it in a particularly readable way. The human components of this mess are detailed in any library, from the stupidity, duplicity, and connivances (see Barbara Tuchman's Pulitzer Prize–winning *Guns of August*) to the pistol shots (fired around noon on June 28, 1914, by Gavrilo Princip) that killed Austrian archduke Francis Ferdinand and his wife, Sophie. Even rational people read today of the ethnic hatred that seethes throughout the Baltic region and note with sadness the same nationalist emotions that sent those bullets into Ferdinand and Sophie, and the same geographic and ethnic names—Bosnia, Serbia—still fuel the bitter and seemingly insoluble conflict in Eastern Europe. But rational people realize that we are not living the book of Revelation. Instead, we are living with our inability to trust and respect one another's lifestyle, culture, genetic heritage, and religion.

DAILY AND FUTURE JUDGMENT DAYS

Although the truly big days of reckoning evidently have not arrived yet, the average American life is filled with small ones: the day on which your divorce becomes final, your child's driver's license test day, and any day upon which our acts of the past days, weeks, months, or years will be judged. Of course we can't determine whether that judgment was by God, the IRS, the divorce court, or a smart-aleck sister-in-law who just managed to find the nastiest and most insulting card for your fiftieth birthday. After fifty, there are no more days of reckoning disguised as birthdays.

The end of the world and the Second Coming continue to be important matters both to theologians and to common citizens. December 31, 1999, is tailor made for the end of the world as we know it, the Second Coming of Christ, judgment, and beginning of the Messianic Millennium. What makes December 31, 1999, so different and dangerous, compared to December 31, 999 (or December 31, 1094, the end of the millennium after Revelation was written), is the global communication network that is one of the results of Adam and Eve's original sin (eating the fruit of the Tree of Knowledge). Thus we've provided ourselves with a tool for multiplying the power of hypnotic body language specialists. This power would not be so dangerous had it not been demonstrated repeatedly that human beings will believe almost anything, especially if they concurrently pray for whatever it is they are being asked to believe.

Our global communication network greatly increases the probability that, as an organic mass, humanity's irrational majority will get duped into thinking that their self-made mess is God's will and that the kindly gentleman smiling from their video screen and asking for money is actually God's chosen messenger. Maybe, in order to put this anticipated event into perspective, we should consider a real day of reckoning that looms on the foreseeable horizon.

The major reckoning day, of course, is the one upon which we run out of crude oil. Scientific predictions about the exact date of this event range from the near future, 2030, to the more distant, around 2100 to 2200. Like all predictions, this one is vulnerable to unforeseen events that increase the rate of global petroleum use (war and advertising), as well as those that decrease this rate (energy taxes, good sense, enlightened public policy, technological breakthroughs). The only certainty is a rather abstract one that most citizens pass off as a jaundiced academic view, namely that modern agriculture has accomplished the conversion of crude oil into people on a massive scale and that when the oil runs out, so will the Earth's capacity for supporting such a population.

Our present petroleum supplies are a product of vast algal beds laid down and buried mainly during the Mesozoic, millions of years ago. Modern agriculture has succeeded in tapping this source of energy—actually fossil sunlight—to produce relatively massive quantities of food. People eat food, grow, have babies that also need food and shelter and eventually have their own babies. Much of the world's food supply comes from farms on which petroleum-driven tractors plant and harvest, petroleum-based chemicals control insects, and petroleum-driven engines pump water for irrigation. Grain is dried, often using electricity from oil or coal-burning plants, then transported by trucks, trains, and ships that all burn petroleum.

Although most of the world's human beings are in a state of denial, at some point in history, we will exhaust this supply of fossil sunlight. After that time, the most likely survivors will be the agrarian people, such as Asian peasants, who still plant crops by hand and fertilize them with their own feces.

Most Christian theologians are fairly empathetic people. They tend to want to relieve human suffering. Although a goodly number of them feel that all human suffering would be relieved if only all humans would accept Jesus as their personal savior, others try to be a little more Earthly and practical in their pronouncements. Among the latter are those who make such statements as: "The problem isn't human population, it's the distribution of food. There's room on Earth for every human being destined to be born. We just need to be more efficient in our distribution of food." This kind of talk is heard most frequently from celebate Catholic bishops.

A lot of businessmen are equally naive, as well as heavily involved in organized religion, and tend to not only agree with celebate Catholic bishops, but to also compound the long-term problem with such dumb and irresponsible utterances as "There's no shortage of oil. We have an oil glut." They are speaking, of course, of this week, this year, and if things go right, this decade.

My personal view is that anyone who listens to Catholic bishops and businessmen on matters of population control and long-term fossil fuel supplies is relatively undereducated. It is true that we have an oil glut (at the time of this writing). And, it is probably true that if all available food supplies and food growth potential were spread evenly throughout the world, virtually everybody would have enough to eat (at the time of this writing). It is also true that petroleum supplies, fresh water, and land are limited resources against which humanity is multiplying exponentially (at the time of this writing). Something, eventually, will have to give. Fundamentalist theologians will welcome the disaster as a sign that all the Biblical prophecies are coming true (once more). Rational people, if any remain, will be left wondering why, why in all living hell, were we not able to solve our strictly human problems using all the enormous human resources on planet Earth?

In summary, there is currently plenty of misery and evil on Earth to consider the 1990s as the final days before the Millennium, but then that same statement could have been made about almost any decade in recorded history. There's always the possibility that this book is way off base and that on December 31, 1999, the world will indeed end. If the Four Horsemen do show up on New Year's Eve, it will likely take a very discerning person to distinguish between the real, prophesied, biblical Revelation and a human one, produced, as so many have been in the past, by irrational people in positions of great power. Indeed, a careful look at history makes one wonder whether what the Bible is really telling us, indirectly, is not to let irrational human beings get into positions of great power if we want to preserve the Eden that used to be planet Earth.

THREE

WESTERN CHRISTIANITY

THE GODS OF WESTERN CHRISTIANITY

Modern Western Christianity has three Gods: the God of the Big Bang, the God of the Mind, and Jesus of Television. These three deities correspond only approximately to God of the Old Testament (i.e., God the Omnipotent), the Holy Spirit, and Jesus. At least two of these gods are very much alive, well, and active. The third, God of the Big Bang, is a legitimate item for philosophical discussion. You might be a rampant atheist, but enough people believe in these gods, and act on their beliefs, to influence your chances of survival past midnight, December 31, 1999.

The God of the Big Bang is the god that created the universe. We have no way of knowing whether this god is real, alive, or well. Some questions are beyond the capacity for human beings to answer (as of this writing), and this is one of them: Did a god create the universe? Science has legitimatized this question, largely through the application of mathematics to observations on radiation and matter, including visible light and subatomic particles, respectively. As we approach the millennium, this question—Did a god create the universe?—is the rough equivalent of some other questions, no doubt asked at other times in history, which at the time were beyond our capacity to answer. For example: What are the stars? For the people who invented the constellations, the answer was a legitimate and widely accepted one: The stars are dots that form images of importance to my culture. For the people who make computers and nuclear missiles (us), the question Did God create the universe? also has a seemingly legitimate and widely accepted answer: Yes. Well-educated people, including theologians, understand that this answer has exactly the same relationship to the universe as Orion, Ursa Major, and Cassiopeia have to the stars. Furthermore, such people also understand that their "yes" answer has a legitimate function for them, just as Orion, Ursa Major, and Cassiopeia had for the ancients.

The God of the Mind is the god that lives in the minds of believers. In this regard, God of the Mind is as alive, well, and active as all other such gods have been throughout recorded history. We don't know whether God of the Mind is, *in fact*, God of the Big Bang. There are many staunch believers in whose minds God lives, and who claim that the two gods are the same. But in the next breath, they'll tell you that evolution is a humanist myth, likely the work of Satan, and a manifestation of original sin in which man ate of the Tree of Knowledge (at the urging of woman and snake). Reasonably well educated rational people know that the God of the Big Bang set up the conditions under which evolution was inevitable.

God of the Mind is a god who has an enormous range of powers and abilities. He/She/It can be benign, or a positive, strengthening force, or a destructive and malignant force. That is, God of the Mind has some of the characteristics of a brain tumor. Religion is an ever-present and socially important factor in human life, largely because God of the Mind is alive and well in so many of us. At Its best, God of the Mind turns us into compassionate, understanding, helpful, tolerant people. At Its worst, God of the Mind turns us into slaves. And who do we become enslaved to? Jesus of Television, of course.

Jesus of Television is a pervasive secular force that we all encounter daily. In preparation for writing this book, I spent hours listening to various orators trying to use Jesus of Television as a power tool. My sequel to *Comes the Millennium* might be a fairly scholarly analysis of this facet of Western Christianity. In brief, Jesus of Television is a hallowed figure who is mostly immune to any kind of negative criticism whatsoever. Anything that the majority of a society agrees is above criticism consequently is immune to control, too. Jesus of Television is pretty much out of control. He's out of control because so many people regard Jesus of Television as Jesus of Nazareth and do not understand the power of choirs; large auditoriums (mob effect); beautiful, clean surroundings; and acting skills to influence their beliefs and actions. Jesus of Television might be Satan in disguise!

I contend that much, if not most, if not the vast majority, of modern Christian evangelism has one goal, admitted or not: the acquisition of power. The formula for acquisition of power is fairly simple: Call on Jesus of Television, use all your acting skills to mine the depths of human self-consciousness in order to equate virtually all natural human behavior with sin, then promise your listeners that Jesus of Television will save them from guilt and sin and give them everlasting life. Now that we've accomplished the salvation of your soul, please send us some money. In my hours and hours of listening to evangelism in preparation for writing this book, I heard very little about the Bible and about religion as a device for helping societies cope with the real problems of having evolved into human societies. What I heard instead was a tiny bit of highly selected scripture used to hammer home the very human message of power: join me completely, subordinate all your human traits to my beliefs, or spend eternity in hell because you were born in sin. Rational people don't believe for one minute that they were born in sin.

In addition to hearing that I was born in sin, I also heard quite a bit of talk about the proper place of women, which is in the home taking care of the children and cooking, cleaning, and washing for a husband. Mowing the grass, too, I suppose, is inferred, but rarely mentioned explicitly.

The last part of this book contains some advice and recommendations, although rational people don't really need such advice. Nevertheless, I'll anticipate that part of the book by suggesting that instead of listening to any dingbat tell you to feel guilty about waking up in the morning as a healthy human being, go to the library and check out some good nonfiction literature on Hebrew, Persian, Roman, and early Christian history. My guess is that after a few Sundays spent reading, in addition to, or even instead of, going to church, you'll feel better about your own personal religious beliefs. But you'll also be frightened about what you see and hear being done in the name of Western Christianity. Suddenly Jesus of Television will begin to look suspiciously like a human construction, specifically a human male construction, that makes you feel enormously guilty but at the same time feeling good about feeling guilty because you know you can be saved.

WESTERN CHRISTIANITY AND SURVIVAL

There are many good reasons why Western, and especially American, Christianity with its three gods, is of vital importance to our survival past midnight, December 31, 1999. These reasons have nothing to do with rapture, salvation, sin, or other theological concepts or phenomena. They have everything to do with the United States having most of the world's guns, controlling most of the world's energy supplies, having a military that is thoroughly infused with Western Christianity, and having inhabitants with a record of behaving as if we consider ourselves God's chosen people. And perhaps most tellingly, we've demonstrated beyond a shadow of a doubt that we're ready, willing, maybe even eager, to use the guns to maintain our control over the energy, especially when that energy is in the hands of non-Western non-Christians. Regardless of how explosive such concoctions made of weapons, religion, and self-righteousness may be in other parts of the world, we have a fairly volatile mix right here in the good ole U.S.A., made more dangerous by the massive supply of all three.

Western Christianity is, of course, based on the Bible, which is a relatively difficult book to read. In order to read the Bible with understanding, one must deal with strange names, foreign cultures, convoluted sentence structure, archaic grammar, symbolism, metaphor, parable, history, poetry, genealogy, mysticism, mythology, the failure, foibles, and conveniences of translators, and the morality tale as a literary device. Moreover, most Bibles have a lot of small print and very few pictures. For all these reasons, a great many of us tend to believe what others tell us the Bible says. Strange names, foreign cultures, convoluted sentence structures, archaic grammar, symbolism, metaphor, parable, history (translated numerous times), poetry, and mythology are not the stock in trade of the American reading public. Indeed, the American public seems to consume far more televised game shows and romance novels than it does literature as sophisticated as the Bible. Someone is deluding someone if we believe that a public whose literary capacity maxes out at Danielle Steel suddenly becomes downright professorial when it picks up a Bible. If true, that is a modern miracle equivalent to any other of the Biblical miracles.

Because (1) the Bible is an extraordinarily powerful piece of *literature*, and (2) very few people actually study the nature and source of Bible stories, Western Christianity allows the power of the Bible to be used by people who claim to explain it. Frequently, if not commonly, such people resort to literal interpretation of the Bible as the most convenient way to explain the Good Book. The easiest explanation of anything written, including the Bible, is an explanation that attributes literal meaning to the words. The creation story of Genesis 1:1–31 is an example of a beautiful myth that untold numbers of people have swallowed hook, line, and sinker. People who take the Genesis creation story literally are simply incapable of making the distinction between religion, history, and fairy tale. They also write letters to *Time* magazine claiming that dinosaurs never existed. It's the fairy tale entitled Revelation, however, that brings into focus our collective gullibility and poses a hazard for all of us as we near the end of the current millennium.

For those who intend to survive beyond midnight, December 31, 1999, it is relatively important to understand the various explanations for statements of any kind, especially those written hundreds of years ago and published in a book as filled with metaphor and allegory as the Bible. Literalists have a particularly fun time with Revelation, possibly because of the rich, fascinating, and thoroughly modern (special-effects) imagery. Among all the evils that fundamentalist Christians and well-meaning United States senators heap on Hollywood, special effects might be appropriately placed at the top of the list. The film artists who brought you *Blade Runner, Aliens,* and *Terminator II* make the verbal descriptions of Revelation seem almost mild, if not actually plausible. I'm speculating, of course, but nevertheless wondering whether Hollywood has made the job easier for those men who choose to use Revelation as a means of bringing others under their power.

WESTERN CHRISTIANITY AND HOLLYWOOD

Western Christianity has much in common with Hollywood. Any carefully done study of biblical history reveals that much, if not most, of the Bible is largely fictitious, with only loose connections to recorded events. My recommendation for reading is a pair of books by Robin Lane Fox, entitled *Pagans and Christians* and *The Unauthorized Version.* Fox is an Oxford historian who examines many of the most basic biblical narratives, from the Exodus to the burning bush to the Nativity, in light of the available evidence to support their actual occurrence. What Fox finds is an enormous amount of truth contained in stories that are not literally true. That is, he finds exactly what any reader finds in a good novel, namely, a commentary on the human condition, a morality lesson, and advice, all built from social and environmental elements familiar to readers. Unlike the vast majority of easily accessible Christian literature, Fox's books are very well documented with references you can check up on, provided you have access to an adequate library and can read Greek.

In order to tell its morality tales, the Bible's authors relied heavily on violence, greed, theft, duplicity, fornication, adultery, death, motherhood, lost children, miracles, politics, war, hallucination, misery, happiness, music, poetry, hope, and food. That is, the Bible deals with about the same list of subjects as the daytime soaps. Most of these phenomena are experienced by non-human primates with, insofar as we know, the exception of hope, music, poetry, miracles, and hallucination (although we don't really know all the pharmacological effects of various plants consumed by monkeys and apes in nature). Miracles and hallucinations may be closely related, the latter being an explanation for the former. A rational scientist familiar with the behavior of monkeys and apes would say that among all the general subjects used by biblical authors to tell their morality tales, only music, poetry, and hope are well documented, clearly and uniquely human entities. Music and poetry can be notoriously blasphemous and heretical, and the best way to eliminate such heresy from music and poetry is to make them focus on hope. The ultimate Western Christian hope, of course, is everlasting life in heaven. Although it's a minor point, we now have an explanation for "Christian Rock" music.

Hollywood may eventually catch on to the natural link between special effects and the book of Revelation. Many mainstream films have been made about Biblical subjects *(The Ten Commandments, The Greatest Story Ever Told, The Last Temptation of Christ)*, but to my knowledge, none yet on the book of Revelation. When such a film is made, America's reaction will be interesting to watch. Conservative Christians, including mainline Baptists and Catholics, are often at the forefront of outraged citizenry's battle against violence and sex on television and in popular films. Rational people will find *Revelation: The Movie* a curious mix of extreme violence coupled with fantasy, all painted with ostensible legitimacy because it's "based on the Bible." Alternatively, however, lay and presumptive Biblical experts might dispute the film's accuracy, having imagined the events in Revelation in ways different from those of the producers and special effects artists. Rational people are likely to view *Revelation: The Movie*, as a population level psycho-wacko experience that might actually be dangerous to society.

Numerous recent films have spawned audience violence, most notably those depicting the brutal lives of minorities confined to inner city ghettos. Perhaps the next non-Bible understanding fundamentalist Christian president and commander-in-chief will be able to nickname his favorite military adventure after still another popular movie. Instead of calling his trillion-dollar fiasco Star Wars, he can call it Revelation, or name his missiles Rapture. Only God knows what kinds of weapons the American public is likely to buy into then, given the financial success of *Revelation: The Movie*, and the resultant catch-phrase power of the film's title.

THE APOCRYPHA

Rational people who are concerned about the Millennium are advised to again consult their local libraries on the book of Revelation, as well as that section of some Bibles (the complete and relatively scholarly ones) entitled the Apocrypha. The writings usually combined under the Apocrypha are those that didn't match up to some of the early codifiers' standards; that is, they might have been seen as heretical. However, the Apocrypha are also possibly just those books that were not part of the pre-Christian Hebrew canon. Whatever they are or are not, Cambridge University Press's *New English Bible* contains the Apocrypha as a separate section, translated and edited (in violation of Revelation's warning?) into an easily accessible text. Maybe I should say the text is easily accessible for a rational person who is accustomed to reading large novels with fine print and no pictures.

The Apocrypha consists of those writings that were primarily accepted by the Greek-speaking, as opposed to the Hebrew-speaking, Jews in Egypt. Before about A.D. 1500, the Apocrypha were distributed throughout the Old Testament. Nowadays, you can buy Bibles with or without the Apocrypha, and if with, then distributed or not distributed throughout the Old Testament. At the forthcoming millennium, as in past millennia, there is no such thing as *the* Bible; there is *a* Bible, which undergoes evolution just like all plants, animals, microbes, rumors, innovations, government agencies, and large, heavily used documents that guide human behavior (e.g., the United States Constitution).

The Apocrypha is a gold mine of Biblical evidence for the fundamental evil of humanity. Gullible Western Christians might ask for the evidence that ". . . not content with gross error in their knowledge of God, men live in the constant warfare of ignorance and call this monstrous evil peace. They perform ritual murders of children and secret ceremonies and the frenzied orgies of unnatural cults" (*Wisdom of Solomon*, 14:22–24). Ritual sacrifice, and the subsequent eating, of children is sometimes thought to occur in Satanic cults (see *The New Yorker*, May 17 and May 24, 1993). Murder, in some cases of children, has been carried out by people claiming their souls belonged to Satan. The murder part of these cases is true and certainly the perpetrator *acted* as if he/she was an agent of Satan. Real murders typically involve some evidence of the crime. And while there are plenty of people *claiming* or *believed* to be possessed by Satan, there's precious little evidence of Satan's presence except in the minds of believers. Thus there may not be a Satan of the Big Bang, but there is certainly a Satan of the Mind and a Satan of Television. Both of these Satans are alive, healthy, and influencing the political, social, and cultural environment in which people try to live safely.

THE LINEARITY OF WESTERN CHRISTIANITY

In addition to having its foundations resting solidly on myth, metaphor, and allegory, especially those involving war, bad women, and violations of the dominance hierarchy, Western Christianity is also highly linear. This linearity permeates the Scriptures as well as the interpretations of those Scriptures in verse, song, and sermon. Furthermore, the linearity occurs at all levels, from the most general to the most specific, from the alpha to the omega form of the Bible, to the tale of the good Samaritan on the road to Damascus. Western Christians seem obsessed with ends, probably because the most staunch believers believe in everlasting life in heaven.

Linearity is one of Christianity's sources of power. With ends come feelings that time is limited and thus certain activities must be done now instead of later. With beginnings and ends, especially those controlled by a supernatural omnipotent being who knows every move we make, even in private, and at the same time can create the universe out of nothing, also comes a sense of purpose and destiny. Thus our job becomes not to solve our problems, but to obey a deity whose landlocked priests are quite capable of explaining virtually anything as being God's will. The promise of everlasting life, which no one has ever been able to prove or disprove, and the threat that everlasting life will be denied unless certain activities have been done, multiplies the power imparted by any linear system for controlling human beings.

Western science is also highly linear. Some philosophers think that the linearity of Western Christianity is one of the major reasons Western science has been so successful at producing items Western Christianity considers the work of Satan.

But Western science has also produced many items Western Christianity relies on very heavily (television, computers, CD players, and so forth). All technology is two-edged. The evilness or holiness of technology depends entirely on the way humans use it. Thus, Pat Robertson can use all of the power of technology and claim his use is sacred, while at the same time decrying Hollywood's use of the same technology as evil.

SATAN TODAY

Most educated people understand that Satan is actually a friend and ally of organized religion, especially that faction of organized religion that wants to use our gullibility to control us. Humans are among the most gullible of animals. They'll believe almost anything and furthermore are prone to fantasy, visions (drug-induced and otherwise), self-deceptions, and various forms of real mental illness. Satan is one of our most persistent visions. This embodiment of evil has stalked Earth for many centuries and has taken many forms. As early as the 4th century A.D., a movement called Manicheism, which sought to explain the large amount of misery in a world supposedly ruled by God, proposed that the Evil Spirit had eternal life equivalent to that of the Good Spirit. Personally, I thought that was a fairly rational, albeit illusionary, way to describe certain primate behaviors. Regardless of how rational such a metaphor seems to us today, the Roman emperor Justinian rewarded such beliefs with the death penalty.

Females have been particularly associated with Satan, along with art. Thus, nude classical Greek statues were often destroyed by Christian Roman emperors. During Christianity's first thousand years, hell was a palpable place, made more so by detailed descriptions of it by people who'd never been there and assumed, because of their beliefs, that they never would. Hell's fires were real, and sulfur was tossed into the flames to generate a stench. Anyone was likely to encounter Satan himself almost anywhere, but he could be frightened away by the sign of the cross. Although the devil was chief womanizer, he had a gang of like-minded demons who crawled into the sack with lonely, as well as holy, women. These Satanic henchmen were capable of all kinds of cruel jokes: making women repulsive to mortal men, thereby causing impotence; stealing semen from potent men and using it to fertilize women who were strangers to them, and so on. Nowadays it costs money to get sperm from a sperm bank. People have always been able to sell themselves to Satan.

In the following chapters, I examine some of the devils that Western Christianity would have us believe walk the earth. These devils take the familiar forms of art, science, sex, etcetera. They are the symbols of a permissive and humanist (read sinful and decadent) society, the kind of society that will be destroyed when the Lord returns at the end of the millennium and either creates Heaven-on-Earth or takes His believers to heaven. My intent in examining these devils is to put them into some kind of a global perspective. In general, we'll find that they've always been with us, that they haven't hurt us very much, and that we've survived many days of reckoning. December 31, 1999, should be just another day in the life of the solar system unless we choose to make it a miserable one.

PART II
SATAN'S WORK

FOUR

ART

SATAN AS A PHOTOGRAPHER

In general, Americans don't seem to care for, appreciate, or even notice art. A remarkable number of well educated people will ignore an original painting or sculpture in a public place unless the artwork blocks the entrance to their office. In the past decade in the United States, however, art has probably aroused the conservative emotions as effectively as any other human product. The pieces involved are a few photographs by two artists, Robert Mapplethorpe and Andres Serrano. In the minds of some, these photographs are clearly the work of Satan, and their display resulted in an explosion of moral indignation, lawsuits, firings of appointed government officials, new federal laws, and much political mileage for ultraconservatives like Senator Jesse Helms.

Rational people asked themselves how and why these few pictures were able to acquire such power and evoke such hostility. The only answer that seemed to be forthcoming was that public funds had been spent to display the offensive photographs. It's not clear whether this art would have been considered the work of Satan had no federal money been involved. Indeed, the most stunning result of Mapplethorpe and Serrano photograph exhibitions was a move, in Congress, to eliminate funding for the National Endowment for the Arts. Had no federal money been involved, people who didn't know or like Serrano or Mapplethorpe probably would have ignored their work, just like people who don't like Picasso and Pollock tend to ignore their work.

I don't know exactly how many Mapplethorpe photographs were involved in this rather illuminating controversy. At least one showed a man with a bullwhip handle sticking into his rectum. This picture probably stirred up a lot of unpleasant memories for United States senators and fundamentalist ministers who'd had hemorrhoid surgery or even an extensive colon exam. One of Mapplethorpe's photographs was purported to be child pornography, or so the lawsuits claimed. So there are at least two Mapplethorpe photographs involved, and just to be on the safe side, let's add seven more. Most of Mapplethorpe's photographs are of simple elegant subjects: flowers and nude black men. Not everyone thinks he was a great artist. But then not everyone likes Picasso, either. The Serrano piece was a single photograph entitled *Piss Christ*, showing a crucifix in Serrano's urine. Serrano is a relative unknown, compared to Mapplethorpe and Picasso. As a result of conservative outrage, *Piss Christ* may go down in history as Andres Serrano's only work of significance to society as a whole. In fact, due largely to that outrage, *Piss Christ* has become virtually iconographic (see *Time* magazine, August 7, 1995). Serrano is probably smiling.

To my knowledge no one has estimated the amount of money various government agencies spent dealing with the controversies aroused by these relatively few photographs. A quick check of the World Book Encyclopedia annual supplement volumes covering the period 1989–1992 suggests that figure is fairly high. I'm going to guess $1 million, although I'd not be surprised if the figure is ten times that much. Satan works in mysterious ways. He makes us spend massive amounts of our money trying to keep from spending a little bit on things we don't like. The fact that Mapplethorpe was a homosexual may have had something to do with Satan's power to make us do such things. I don't know anything about Serrano's sexual orientation. Obviously he was not overly enamored with the Catholic Church, a trait he shares with numerous people in Mexico and Northern Ireland.

How many pictures do humans take every year? It's hard to estimate. But I take a lot of photographs myself and have traveled fairly extensively, including many trips to foreign countries. I see cameras everywhere. The Japanese alone probably take more pictures, by three orders of magnitude, than one would estimate based on personal experience alone. I'm going to guess 15 billion photographs a year. But that's only three pictures a year for every person on Earth. The more I think about this estimate, the more I think it undershoots the mark, so to speak, by a long shot. Fifty billion photographs a year would be ten for every person on Earth. Let's go with 50 billion. If Satan's work in the realm of photography consists of *Piss Christ* plus the generous estimate of nine or ten offensive pictures by a now-dead gay man, then any rational person has to ask whether maybe Satan shouldn't have to work a little harder for his hold on our emotions.

OFFENSIVE ART

In general, irrational people among us are not offended by a work of art unless it has some or all of the following characteristics:

1. It is abstract.
2. It is not "pretty." (No one knows, but small groups often agree on, what "pretty" means.)
3. It shows the human body in some stage of undress.
4. It shows some sexual situation ranging from mildly odd to outright criminal.

Why should these attributes characterize a work of Satan? Probably because they are editorials. Although anyone might object to certain displays of art showing outright criminal acts, most rational people will at least analyze the piece, trying to determine the artist's meaning and intent, as well as the context in which the piece was done, before asking that it be removed, destroyed, or become the object of a lawsuit. More often than not, when such works are done by a legitimate artist, they are a commentary on the society in which the artist lives (although the artist may deny such intent). And, they should be viewed as such.

A fifth characteristic—the one exhibited by Andres Serrano's *Piss Christ*—shows religious figures or icons, or even politicians, in less than glorious circumstances. For example, a fairly realistic painting entitled *Jesus Leaving the Outhouse* would be sure to elicit strong reactions from many people regardless of whether federal money was spent on it. Similarly, a life-sized bronze nude sculpture entitled *Jesus Studying His Ingrown Toenail* would likely elicit an outcry from the moralists. But those same people often refer to Jesus as the "incarnation" (the human body version) of God. You can't be incarnate without defecating and urinating; stuff goes into the human body, gets metabolized into more human body, then comes out. And anyone who's ever walked around in sandals for a couple of years knows that such behavior can produce foot troubles in a hurry. (Unless, of course, the sandals are Birkenstocks.)

The aforegoing discussion of offensive paintings and sculptures dealing with incarnation, bodily functions, and foot trouble are a demonstration of the power of art to quickly and summarily make a statement counter to the wishes of the prevailing power structure. And I haven't even painted the offending picture or sculpted the offending bronze nude. I just put the *idea of a piece of art* into words. We have discovered the source of Satan's power! Art can reach into our minds, into our memories, into our deepest feelings and prejudices and pluck out instantaneous reactions to inanimate objects that are doing us no physical harm.

INTENT OF THE ARTIST

Art, of course, can be defined in countless ways. Indeed, What is art? may be one of the most enduring and unanswerable questions addressed by scholars and consumers alike. Art, like beauty, is often in the mind of the beholder. But that tired cliché is a fairly simplistic view of art, as well as of beauty. As a rational working definition, I suggest that art is anything made by an individual with the intent of making art. If that definition is circular, then so be it. We could, by analogy, say that a machine is anything made by an individual, committee, or corporation with the intent of making a machine. The art doesn't have to be good, commercially viable, or important. Nor does the machine have to work in the manner intended. I'm defining the product in terms of the intent of the manufacturer. Anyone dissatisfied with that definition can make up his or her own—for both art and machinery. I'm guessing he or she will struggle with those definitions just like others have done for a long long time. Eventually, we all come back to the matter of intent.

A coat hanger bent on purpose to retrieve some object from an inaccessible place is a tool. The worst home video or a child's first sloppings with fingerpaint might well be art. But both these items are at the lower commercial and critical end of the machinery/art spectrum. Found metal objects, welded together to make a Deborah Butterfield horse, for example, are near the upper end of the spectrum. Such intended constructions stand in some of the nation's finest art museums. Similarly, Louise Nevelson's blocks of wood—arranged, affixed to one another, and painted—also adorn the walls of some of our finest museums (as well as the Seattle airport). Neither Ms. Butterfield nor Ms. Nevelson did a whole lot more than "bend a coat hanger" in order to make their art, but they applied some intangible, unquantifiable quality of their minds—an inner personal vision— to their intended constructions. We can thus define "successful artist" much more easily than we can define "art." Successful artists are those whose intentions, manifested as tangible objects, communicate in an intangible way with a relatively large number of other human beings. Sales tend to confirm this definition.

ART AS EXPLORATION

Art, like science, is an effort on the part of individual human beings to explore the world in which they live. The exploration methods of artists are different from those of scientists, but art is exploration nevertheless. Artists explore vision, values, attitudes, and the communication power of pattern. Most artists don't think in such formal terms, especially when they do their work. Instead, artists make art. Interpretations are most often by non-artists, including some very astute people in the business of selling art, as well as some complete fools in high places (see the information in your local library about Richard Serra's *Tilted Arc* during the middle 1980s). I've never been able to figure out why some people exhibit such emotional anti-art feelings, especially over abstract art. These feelings come out as demeaning, insulting statements about the quality of the art and ridicule for the artist. Often the ridicule is accompanied by the statement "I could have done that!"

One museum staff member I talked to said that if the people who ridiculed art "could have done that," then why didn't they do it? Then she said, "I'll tell you why they don't do art. Those people are mental slaves to a literal view of the world in which there are no shades of gray, no paradoxes, no open-ended questions, no unsolvable controversies." Then she said she felt sorry for people who couldn't tolerate and appreciate someone else's efforts, whether they liked the results of those efforts or not.

I know a great many artists, some very successful financially and in terms of critical acclaim. Most of these artists are kind, sensitive, intelligent, but rather focused, individuals. They are technically skillful, some enormously so (e.g., those who work with watercolors or heavy metal). I don't think any of them actively try to paint pictures or take photographs or make sculptures because these works have commercial value. They tend to put their work on display because that's what artists do, and sometimes the artists are happy when it sells. Artists are not always pleased to part with their pieces. I suppose when you run out of coffee, then it's time to sell a painting, but most of the artists I know are fairly protective about their work. To a person, however, there is one question the artists I know would never ask: Should I paint this picture, knowing full well it will offend someone? Instead, these artists ask questions like Where did I put that small flat brush? and Why didn't I remember to buy some more red ocher yesterday? It's not a matter of caring or not caring about those in positions of political and social power. Most artists never think about the tyrants until it's too late.

ART HISTORY

Art historians and critics, on the other hand, do a lot of thinking about social impacts and statements of artists. Furthermore, their thinking is not limited to this week's scandal or yesterday's obscenity. Art historians, especially the best ones, examine the political and social events of times past and present, in cultures American and non-American, and try to evaluate artists' contributions to their own and later cultures. In other words, historians and critics ask, What is the artist saying? Sometimes the historians and critics make sense, sometimes they don't. But the best ones are like the better scientists in that they make sense more often than not. And, just like scientists and other professional people, the critics disagree among themselves. In general, however, they agree on one thing: Art, like prayer, never hurt anyone.

Art is primarily a reflection of its times, not vice versa. A work of art is a summary of the artistic technology and "vocabulary" of the era in which the piece was made. In addition, a work of art is the unique application of that technology and the unique use of that "vocabulary" by the artist. This is why historians and critics also generally agree that art, in contrast to the public and official government record, is one of the more authentic cultural reflections of its times. But the *interpretation* of that reflection, just like our interpretations of the Bible's reflections of ancient Hebrew, Roman, and Persian cultures, or of our own reflection in the mirror, is a product of our times. Art of such quality that it inspires efforts to interpret it over long periods of time—Michelangelo Buonarroti's frescoes or the paintings of Rembrandt—is considered "good" and important, and rightfully so. Art that possesses certain qualities that inspire extensive and fairly immediate efforts to interpret it also is important. An example of such art is the body of American Abstract Expressionist painting that so many literalists find incomprehensible or offensive (probably because it's incomprehensible to them).

Those who cannot "understand" abstract, nonliteral, or otherwise "offensive" art are really those who are uncomfortable in the absence of authority. No one can really "understand" such art. Instead, you have to open up your mind, appreciate the work as a unique product of a unique mind and body, ask yourself what the artist might have intended, and ask yourself what the piece "says" to you regardless of its other properties. That is, you have to participate, as an individual interpreter, in the individual act of the artist.

Interpretation is generally what people with a strong need to be part of a dominance hierarchy crave from others. They are reluctant to interpret much of anything on their own and seek out others to interpret their world—including the news, the Bible, art, music, and science—for them. In the final analysis, this is the basis for considering art to be the work of Satan. For those for whom individual interpretation is anathema, art

can be the ultimate challenge to their guiding authority. Works
of art are, in the final analysis, statements by individual human
beings that they themselves bring something to this world regardless of how much pleasure, pain, or satisfaction they also
bring to any president, senator, dictator, CEO, or god.

FIVE

SCIENCE

Ever since the codification of Christianity, science has been considered the work of Satan. Indeed, out of all the historical narratives describing humanity's struggles with itself, the conflict between science and religion, especially Western Christian religion, is the best documented and most clearly indicative of social behaviors destructive to both society and the individuals involved. One of the surest ways to get killed during the Dark Ages was to suggest a natural explanation or cause for *anything* that contradicted what people believed the Scriptures said about the same phenomenon. The literary sources to support this assertion are voluminous, easily available, widely distributed, widely read and understood, and in terms of familiarity, almost walking-around knowledge of educated people. Once inside a typical public library, it might take a high school student three minutes to find several references to scientists being executed for suggesting things we all take for granted today (e.g., the Earth is round and orbits the sun).

It's a waste of time to present one more litany of unenlightened behavior on the part of organized religion during the nearly two millennia between the classical Greeks and the Renaissance. The tragedy, as well as a major factor contributing to the self-fulfilling nature of end-of-the-world prophecies is that this irrational and unenlightened behavior still persists. Every creationist's letter to the editor, decrying the teaching of evolution, is evidence that such behavior still persists. And every time massive crowds descend upon some poor hamlet where a stressed-out woman has had a vision of the Virgin Mary on the side of the town water tower, that is evidence that humans will believe virtually anything.

Science can't explain everything . . . yet. Indeed, the hallmark of science is that the more it learns about nature, the more questions it uncovers about nature. In the course of discovering explanations, science also discovers questions. This is the fundamental property of science and any claim to the contrary reveals an enormous ignorance of basic scientific principles. Ronald Reagan is an excellent example of an elected leader who had no understanding whatsoever of science, the contributions science makes to a developed nation, the origin of human resources to conduct the scientific enterprise, and the philosophical and ethical ramifications of scientific research. Instead, Reagan considered science a tool of government, especially an economic and military tool.

THE ORIGIN OF SCIENTISTS

When presidents consider science to be an economic and military tool, then they act as if they believe scientists spring fully formed from the adult male population whenever needed by a nation to fight a war or a disease or invent something useful. Nothing could be further from the truth. Science does not necessarily emerge fully formed from even a well-educated society, nor do scientists themselves suddenly appear upon military or economic demand. Both science and practicing scientists must be developed over a long period. The insight necessary to design experiments, build new scientific equipment, ask the right questions, and see the potential for advancement where others are blind cannot be taught in school. Instead, these traits must be allowed to develop in individuals who practice science, making their mistakes along the way, but always, *always*, trying first to satisfy their own curiosity.

The satisfaction of one's curiosity is often perceived, especially in political and economic circles, as an elitist luxury. In America, people *work*, and work *hard;* they don't sit around trying to figure out how nature operates, especially when such activity seems to contradict Biblical admonitions. Yet it is this very search, conducted broadly by a relatively large segment of the population, that assures a nation its scientific and technological resources will be available when needed.

A nation's scientific enterprise cannot be ridiculed by politicians for not attacking what those politicians see as the most crucial and immediate problems. Politicians are not scientists. Politicians never make scientific discoveries. Politicians seek political power and use every means at their disposal to obtain the approval of their constituency. All of this perfectly normal political behavior violates the finest traditions of science and in fact destroys science when scientists practice it. Technology is not science, but it is derived from science. We all use technology. The drugs we take, cars we drive, television sets we turn on, bar codes we see on virtually every piece of merchandise are all technological products of the scientific enterprise. Technology provides power both to individuals, such as politicians and televangelists, *and* to societies.

TECHNOLOGY

One of the major problems of a scientifically illiterate society is that its leaders are often unable to distinguish between science and technology. A large number of people in responsible positions who should know better think that science and technology are the same. They aren't. Technology is a human activity that intends to produce something of use to humans.

Technology relies on scientific explanation as a source of raw material. Engineers are generally not scientists; they are technologists trying to solve practical problems. Such solutions are the source of power. Small wonder that "technology transfer" is a catchphrase one hears often in economists' and politicians' discussions of science.

Organized religion rarely considers engineers and technologists to be Satanic. In fact, organized religion relies heavily on the tools technologists make from discovered explanations. Such tools include wireless microphones, television cameras, transmitters and receivers, fax machines, computers, airplanes, and a large array of medical equipment and procedures owned and conducted by denominational hospitals. Technologists have made organized religion powerful and in some cases rich. Scientists, on the other hand, have generally made organized religion mad, mainly because science negates the "God did it" explanation for natural phenomena. Organized religion does not want to be told that "God didn't do it" by the same people who've ultimately made possible global communications networks, the medical procedures used daily in Catholic and Baptist hospitals, and computers used to keep track of church money.

A deeply religious person is perfectly capable of holding to the "God did it" explanation if such a person accepts that God works in many and mysterious ways. In fact, there is probably not a minister on Earth, fundamentalist Christian or not, who hasn't occasionally admitted that God works in many and mysterious ways. Any God of the Big Bang obviously has the capacity to work in exactly the same way as scientists claim nature works. God of the Big Bang ought to be perfectly capable of making the approximately spherical (instead of flat) Earth revolve around the Sun (instead of vice versa) or, for that matter, making the dinosaurs evolve, then become extinct. Needless to say, there is a staggering amount of theological leeway that an educated person has for reconciling his or her religious beliefs with the discoveries of science.

SCIENTISTS' VIEW OF THE MILLENNIUM

There are very few claims that make scientists laugh more readily than the claim that the Millennium is upon us, that all the sinners will be destroyed and sent to hell, that Jesus will return, and that the rapturous saved will live in a thousand-year heaven on Earth. To scientists, some of the modern apocalyptic literature is simply ludicrous. One example is the perfectly dumb book entitled *Armageddon: Appointment with Destiny*, by Grant R. Jeffrey, published in 1988 by Bantam Books in New York City. Mr. Jeffrey evidently bought a new MacIntosh computer and decided to try out its graphics and map programs to put together this piece of tripe. Remember those records in which a voice like Senator Everett Dirksen's went through this long comic narrative built on the fact that "Kennedy" and "Lincoln" have the same number of letters? This is the essence of Grant Jeffrey's *Armageddon*. On the other hand, the truly frightening possibility is that *Armageddon* was bought in fairly large numbers by people who (1) believed this garbage and (2) behaved in a way that increased, rather than decreased, the world's problems. After all, Hal Lindsey's book *The Late Great Planet Earth*, a pop-apoc uncle to *Armageddon*, went through fourteen printings in the early 1970s. One should never underestimate this nation's supply of gullibility; if we could bottle the stuff and sell it, we'd all be rich. Come to think of it, Grant Jeffrey and Hal Lindsay have done just that.

Another piece of garbage that I found quickly in my local library was Theodor Reik's 1957 book *Myth and Guilt: The Crime and Punishment of Mankind*, published by George Braziller, Inc., also of New York. Mr. Reik's book contains the sentence "The biblical story of Noah preserves thus the memory of the Ice Age and of the Flood resulting from the melting of the glaciers." Someone should tell Mr. Reik that the glaciers were already melted down to near their present condition when the 600-year-old Noah built his ark in 2400 B.C. (based on Asimov's estimate of the date, which is in turn based on the admittedly wrong figure of 4004 B.C. for the origin of the universe). Someone also should tell Mr. Reik that most geologists feel that when the glaciers melted, the result was much the same as it is today when glaciers melt. Instead of a biblical Noah-type flood, we get fine rivers with abundant water for agriculture. Besides, the Bible says rain caused the flood, not melting glaciers.

The Flood story is a great piece of fiction and a nice morality tale, probably plagiarized, stolen, or borrowed from earlier Sumerian folktales or from any of the many similar myths in numerous cultures. But why did Noah take along parasites, mosquitoes, rattlesnakes, cockroaches, flies, and many other obnoxious animals? Either he didn't take them and they evolved since the flood, or he did take them for some reason not explained in the Bible except that God told him to take at least one pair of every living kind (and seven pairs of the ritually clean kinds of animals). Is it possible that Noah took seven pairs of tapeworms by accident, not knowing they were inside the seven pairs of ritually (but not necessarily veterinarily) clean animals? Does that mean that tapeworms are by Biblical definition ritually clean? And what about the beetles that we're discovering at such a remarkable rate? Scientists sitting around in a local bar might have a blast discussing Noah's struggles to find one pair of the 250,000 species of beetles discovered in the nearly 4,500 years since the flood. Noah was a truly remarkable man. He even found, properly classified, and took along on the Ark a pair each of the estimated million plus species of beetles yet to be discovered (estimate based on the rate we're now discovering them) in the tropical forests of Latin America. Of course there is no mention of Latin America in the Bible. Noah must have gone to the tropics, done all that taxonomy, figured out how to culture these microscopic critters, and gotten them back to the Ark, all without being recorded by the scribes of the day. Most scientists would conclude that the scribes of the day missed a golden opportunity to burnish Noah's image still further by failing to record these remarkable deeds.

My guess is that the more beer these scientists drink, the

more bizarre become their efforts to reconcile Noah's accomplishments with what is known about animal diversity today. These same scientists are likely to become maudlin by the end of the evening, remembering the influence irrational deluvian explanations had on scientists of the 17th and 18th centuries. By the time they get home, they're probably crying because college freshmen in the United States of America still show up in their classes believing the universe was created in 4004 B.C. and resisting all efforts to convince them otherwise. The scientists I've talked to about the state of the world are very depressed over the negative impact fundamentalist Christians have had on American society and on our ability to educate ourselves out of our problems. These same scientists are doubly depressed by the fact that fundamentalist Christians seem to *want* these problems to get worse as a sign Jesus is coming.

FALSIFIABILITY

In order to be scientific, an assertion must be capable of being tested to determine whether it is true or false; that is, it must be falsifiable. The major problem with Christianity, as well as with religion in general, is that, with one exception, the claims made by converts are unfalsifiable. The exception concerns the behavior of believers. The assertion that believers exhibit behaviors consistent with their beliefs is, in fact, testable and therefore meets the first criterion of scientific, as opposed to nonscientific, statements. However, this assertion concerns a natural phenomenon, namely human behavior, rather than a supernatural one such as the behavior of God. Because all natural phenomena can be studied by truly scientific methods, so can the behavior of believers. One can adequately test the prediction, for example, that the most fanatic fundamentalist Christians will discriminate against people different from themselves, exhibit sexist attitudes, commit violent acts in pursuit of their goals, raise money, believe complete lies, and convince them-

SCIENCE   51

selves that the Millennium is at hand. Most of these behaviors can be quite dangerous to society as a whole. In all fairness, fundamentalist Christians are not all bad. It can also be predicted that they will give a lot of money to help people less fortunate than themselves, buy gifts for the needy at Christmas, visit the sick and elderly, conduct funeral services that help people get through stressful times in their lives, counsel alcoholics, visit prisons, and perform a long list of other charitable acts. In addition to their charitable acts, on the other hand, they will object to a long list of books in public and school libraries. Such objections are typically based on sexual content and/or profanity in these books. The problem with fanatical Christians is that so often it is very difficult for them to separate their Christianity from their desire to impose their narrow moral codes on the rest of the world. There is no concrete scientific evidence that such a link should be necessary. A search for such evidence would make a nice doctoral thesis in anthropology.

Most of the rest of organized religion's assertions are untestable, (unfalsifiable), therefore unscientific. Here we have the dangerous essence of the science vs. religion conflict. It is crucial to our survival past midnight, December 31, 1999, that we understand this essence. *Unfalsifiable does not equate with true!* If a statement is unfalsifiable, then it cannot be *tested* for its truth or falsity. Such statements are make believe, fairy tales, myths, lies, conjectures, etc., etc. These statements might be nice and useful lies and fairy tales, but they are just that—fairy tales. They are not fairy tales because they are wrong but because they cannot be tested to determine whether they are wrong. Fairy tales are not necessarily bad for society. What's bad for society are tyrants posing as messiahs and using fairy tales to gain power over uneducated people.

The Bible is full of unfalsifiable stories and unverifiable histories. To list them would require a book almost as big as a Bible. People often believe these tales. Modern advances in psychiatric medicine suggest that much more of human behavior is controlled by body chemistry than once thought. Body chemistry is, in turn, controlled largely by genetic makeup. The truly frightening possibility is that susceptibility to myths and fairy tales is behavior with a strong genetic component. Such a possibility opens up another, namely, that humans *evolved* this trait as a result of some selective events occurring in prehistory. The psychiatrists I talked to before writing this book just shrugged when I suggested that irrationality might be controlled, at least in part, by genetics. I took the shrug to mean so what's so startling about that?

THE MILLENNIUM HYPOTHESIS

I sometimes get asked: *How do you know that Jesus isn't coming to start the Millennium on December 31, 1999?* I don't. No one knows for sure. The assertion that Jesus is coming is an unfalsifiable claim. A falsifiable, therefore testable and non-fairytale claim, however, is that *people will act as if Jesus is coming to start the Millennium on December 31, 1999.* If there is any sure statement one can make about the Millennium, it's that people have believed in it for centuries, have claimed its imminence for centuries, and have been disappointed, also for centuries, that the world did not end on schedule. The Millennium is a highly useful fairy tale borrowed from various noncanonized Hebrew and Sumerian sources by a possibly demented visionary on the Island of Patmos in the Aegean Sea and codified in a hallucinogenic book entitled Revelation. There is one other historical observation of importance in this regard: the failure of a messiah to appear on schedule has routinely been taken as evidence that a *real* messiah is on his/her/its way.

The major usefulness of the Millennium is to frighten uneducated people. Frightened uneducated people are easily dominated and enslaved. This is why the fundamentalist Christian right wants certain books removed from your child's library, why the fundamentalist Christian right wants certain art removed from your local gallery, why the fundamentalist Christian right wants the teaching of evolution eliminated from your child's curriculum, and why, if given the choice, the fundamentalist Christian right would close the public schools entirely.

Here are some legitimate questions raised by intelligent, well-educated people with reasonable religious beliefs:

1. How do you know that Jesus is not coming soon?
2. How do you know that God did not make the universe?
3. How do you know there's no heaven and no hell?
4. How do you know we are not made in God's image?
5. How do you know Christian Americans are not God's chosen people?
6. How do you know that there are not other intelligent civilizations out there in the universe?

The honest answer is I don't, and neither does anyone else, regardless of what they believe. With the exception of item number six, the concepts behind those questions cannot be explored scientifically, therefore they cannot be verified or rejected. Jesus might come tomorrow. God of the Big Bang might well have made the universe. There might well be a heaven and hell, and if so, then as a result of writing this book, I'll see some of you in hell. We don't know whether we are made in God's image. We do know, however, that we are quite capable of constructing a God made in *our* image. We don't know whether we are God's chosen people. We do know that humans everywhere are capable of acting like they are God's chosen people. We don't know whether there are other intelligent civilizations out there. If there are, then I hope we discover them soon. Maybe, just maybe, that discovery will reduce the number of people who are convinced there is only one inhabited planet in the universe, and that that planet is inhabited by people made in God's image. I sincerely hope those intelligent beings from outer space look like dinosaurs and act like my rational, well-educated, tolerant humanist friends. That's my personal fairy tale.

Back to science.

THE PRODUCTS OF SCIENCE

Science is humanity's attempt to explain the universe in nonsupernatural terms. Science produces three things: tools, concepts, and world views. The tools become technology—television, satellites, medical procedures, and weapons. The concepts become guiding abstractions that practicing scientists try to express, test, or explore in tangible terms. Often concepts are presented as ideas: "energy is lost between trophic levels of a food pyramid." That seemingly arcane bit of scientific talk, when converted into a tangible observation, might be expressed as a fact every farmer knows: the food it takes to make a cow weighs more than the cow you end up with. The difference in the weight of the food vs. the weight of the finished cow is "energy lost between trophic levels." Concepts are not political or economic tools, but exploratory tools. Concepts guide research; they are part of the rationale behind decisions to perform certain studies and experiments. Most scientists spend most of their time testing established concepts. A few truly creative scientists spend some of their time looking for new or unexpressed concepts. That is, the most creative scientists are looking for problems rather than answers.

Science and religion clash most strongly over the third product of science—world views. World views are actually universe views; one's world includes one's universe. Expressed simply and bluntly, the two opposing world views are as follows:

> *Religion:* God made the universe and all that's in it.
> *Science:* A god might well be responsible for the Big Bang, but everything post–Big Bang evolved and

developed from that original supply of mass and energy according to laws and principles humans can discover.

In essence, religion demands an active hand of God, while science seeks explanations that do not demand an active and controlling hand of God. It's fun to imagine what God of the Big Bang might actually be like, even given that with the present technology we can't explore the pre-Bang universe very deeply. Even scientists, including some atheistic ones, sit around occasionally and talk about the God of the Big Bang. And, much of this conversation is fairly serious. Scientists are neither above religion, nor immune to it, but their profession makes them exceedingly skeptical of the way religion is often used by their fellow humans.

The two world views—those of religion and science—clash most strongly on the matter of solutions to large human problems, and especially so on the rationale for even seeking solutions to such problems. Thus most scientists feel that it is in our best interests to control human population growth and energy consumption. The religious right, however, rarely if ever addresses these problems, evidently feeling that they are not important ones in comparison to obscene art, homosexuality, and lack of prayer in the public schools.

This difference in viewpoint originates in the scientists' daily experience, which tells them that human beings *do* have the power to solve major practical problems and that human beings *should* apply those powers to the problems we face, as a species, today. The daily experience of the religious right, on the other hand, tells them the Rapture is near so not to worry about anything beyond morals and souls. The scientists' daily experience comes from a regular encounter with the natural forces that govern our existence on this planet. The daily experience of Christian fundamentalists consists mainly of regular encounters with like-minded people. My sense is that on the subject of world views, the scientists are the ones to listen to, not because the Biblical prophecies are all wrong, but because they are so easy to produce on purpose just by listening to like-minded people who convince us to behave in self-fulfilling ways.

SIX

EVOLUTION

I don't intend to try to convince anyone that evolution is a fact. That battle has already been fought, and the evolutionists have won. It doesn't make any difference what anyone *believes*, the brutal truth is that planet Earth has seen a long parade of life-forms that appeared (having evolved from their ancestors) and then disappeared over a three-and-a-half-billion-year period, usually living in wondrous and exotic profusion, flourishing, speciating, and becoming extinct, from the depths of the oceans to the tops of the highest mountains.

If someone wants to *believe* that God reached down from heaven and made Adam in 4004 B.C., then it's that person's perfect right to so *believe*. In fact, anyone has the perfect right to believe virtually anything about everything in the universe. But people who try to force their beliefs on society, at least in the United States of America, should expect some resistance. Why do secular humanists and well-educated people resist certain beliefs? Because if those beliefs are incorporated into national policy, and conflict strongly enough with the beliefs of others in far-off lands, we could easily see our children marching off to a holy war.

So both adults and home-schooled fundamentalist children

are free to believe that God created the universe in seven days. But the scientists, and most well-educated citizens of the realm, know that life on Earth has been evolving for at least 3 billion years. That knowledge does not make well-educated citizens sinners or destroy their family values, nor does it deprive them of moral character. Acceptance of the theories, evidence, and inferences of evolutionary biology does not necessarily make one an adulterer, a homosexual, a thief, a murderer, a rapist, a child molester, a drug dealer, or a communist. Instead, it allows one to view creation myths, including those in the Bible, as wonderfully useful, often beautiful metaphors, which in other times had much redeeming value for society.

Before progressing much further, maybe I should define "evolution" and explain, as best I can, what it means. "To evolve" means to change—permanently and irreversibly. To evolve in the biological sense means for a population to change genetically, at least, and ultimately in form (phenotypically). There is ample evidence that populations—from viruses to human beings—change genetically with time. Darwin himself drew on centuries of animal and plant breeding to document that populations not only change genetically over time, they also can be made to do so on purpose.

With genetic change, comes, eventually, structural or phenotypic change. *Phen-* comes from the Greek word *phainein*, which means to show. Phenotypes are therefore the features that an organism "shows" (i.e., attributes we can see). The word *see*, however, has many meanings to modern science. Technology allows us to see many things we could not have a century ago. So now phenotype can refer to a whole suite of traits, including chemical makeup. But the bottom line is that in evolving populations, genetic changes lead to changes in structure and chemistry of living organisms.

"Speciation" means the generation of new species. Obviously populations can differ genetically and phenotypically without necessarily being different species. Human ethnic diversity is an excellent example of this rule. In order to be different species, the populations also need to be reproductively isolated. That is, they need to be incapable of interbreeding because of their underlying biological properties. These properties are often ones we can see, such as the differences between dogs and cats. Every anti-evolutionist can cite instances in which presumably different species can be made to interbreed, therefore negating science's definition of a species. Every well-educated rational person knows that the study of life is the study of generalities, not certainties. There are many exceptions to hard and fast rules that presumably apply to organisms. You may be able to force two species to interbreed in the lab. If they are closely enough related genetically, they may even interbreed in nature. Such an event does not refute the theories of evolution. It does, however, produce an argument over whether the two "species" should be considered distinct or not. The observation and the argument are sort of routine daily business in biology. But for every such observation and argument, there are thousands of cases in which scientists completely agree on the number, and distinctiveness, of the species involved.

The average citizen never can know of the scientific agreements or the vast and overwhelming majority of plant and animal species that occupy Earth. The average citizen sees a minuscule sample of the larger species, and most of these are vertebrates (sharks, fish, amphibians, reptiles, birds, and mammals or woody shrubs and trees). By "larger" I mean anything larger than an earthworm. Most animals are smaller than an earthworm, and although most plants, especially the flowering plants, are larger, most plants are also in the tropics, where people as a rule don't argue much about creation vs. evolution. In fact, most animals on Earth are hidden away among these topical plants. So when a local American creationist starts talking about evolution, that individual virtually by definition is speaking out of monumental ignorance. Typically such a creationist is ridiculing the idea that evolution could produce a dog by selectively breeding a cat, or some equivalent nonsense, all within the lifetime of the observers. Scientists ridicule such ideas, too, mainly because they are founded on a monumental ignorance.

Evolutionists tend to argue a lot over speciation, especially over the underlying causes and rates. Darwin was convinced that new species arose slowly, mainly through competition. Some naturally occurring variants would out-compete others for limited resources; then over time the "others" would die out. A succession of winners would eventually become different enough from their parent populations to be called new species. Modern evolutionists tend to feel that reproductive isolation, rather than competition, is the major underlying cause of speciation. Populations become separated reproductively then evolve into different species by means of a number of genetic mechanisms well established in the scientific literature. The isolation itself can result from many factors such as mutations, chromosomal events, geological or ecological events.

Darwin came to his conclusions after studying biology for many years, including experimentation and global travel. He also studied agricultural research and concluded that for the past several centuries farmers had used methods virtually identical to his evolutionary ideas to generate new breeds of domestic plants and animals. Modern evolutionary biologists have access to many techniques and much information that Darwin lacked, including genetics and molecular biology, analytical biochemistry, the electron microscope, and computers. The science of statistics, for example, is post-Darwinian (Karl Pearson, usually credited with the development of modern statistical methods was born a year before *Origin of Species* was published). Nor was even elementary genetics, as we know it today, a part of Darwin's intellectual arsenal. In addition, in the early to mid 1800s, there were not very many evolutionary biologists. Today there are hundreds of scientists who study evolution either directly or indirectly. So it should come as no surprise that Darwinian principles and conclusions have been modified. No one is saying that Darwin was basically wrong; many are saying that his story was just incomplete.

Speciation, the generation of new species, is called micro-evolution because it involves small changes (micro). Macro means "large," and evolution that produces large changes (e.g., the production of major groups such as dogs and horses) is called macroevolution. "What events cause horses to evolve into new species of horses?" is a microevolutionary question. "What events resulted in the evolutionary divergence of major groups of mammals, for example, dogs, horses, and bats?" is a macro-evolutionary question. Scientists argue constantly over the mechanisms, timing, and evidence to support various answers to these questions. Scientists never argue over the question of whether horses evolved or were created, *as horses distinct from cows*, by God. Scientists who believe God created horses also believe that God set up the conditions under which present-day horses evolved from their ancestors. Then such scientists, if they are at all interested in evolution, set about to discover the mechanisms by which God allowed horses to evolve from non-horses.

Of course not all scientists are interested in horses. Many are concerned with beetles, butterflies, flowers, and worms that live in the mud. But because they're scientists, they generally accept the fact of evolution and argue about its form, regardless of whether they believe in God or not. None of this intellectual activity turns these people into murderers, rapists, child molesters, communists, or homosexuals. Some of them, however, are registered Democrats.

Evolution is a controversial subject because scientists explain the origin of life, as well as plant and animal diversity, on the basis of evolutionary change, whereas some nonscientists explain life's origin and diversity on other bases, such as special creation by supernatural force (God). The origin of life and diversity is evidently something that people feel strongly about, especially in the United States. In fact, a whole list of subjects are tied to one's view of the origin of life and diversity. A partial list of such subjects might read as follows:

1. Our world view.
2. The purpose of life in general.
3. The purpose of our individual lives.
4. The existence of free will.
5. Morality.
6. Human rights and privileges.
7. The origin of knowledge.
8. What happens to us when we die.
9. The humanness of those who hold views different from ours.
10. The rights and privileges of nonhuman species.
11. The range of possible solutions to major social problems.
12. What we read and who we listen to.

Scientific research suggests answers to the questions raised by these items, and so scientists sometimes have a profound impact on our daily intellectual lives. Science does not, on the other hand, erode the moral, social, and economic foundations of our culture. As is the case with technology, whatever we do with scientific discoveries may erode certain social structures, but even that erosion does not necessarily produce an evil, immoral, degenerate society. Indeed, a case might well be made that a minimum amount of intellectual honesty and objective introspection is good for society.

In that vein, I reiterate: the evolutionists have won. But the human is still a highly spiritual (mystic) and social species. Our personal spiritual lives will not be destroyed by middle school science teachers who tell children the dinosaurs evolved into an amazingly diverse group of animals during the Mesozoic. Most of us do, of course, have the right to jerk our kids out of that school and educate them at home. Exercise of that right, stimulated by a passionate belief that evolution is a lie, is guaranteed to produce an ignorant child. Fortunately, in this day and age, it is easy to be relatively ignorant and still do fairly well on SAT and ACT tests (although a kid needs to know math and

the meanings of many words), so that ignorance will not, by itself, keep a child out of a large public university or even a high
quality private one.

Parents can also send their children to certain Christian col-
leges, which will guarantee that their ignorance about plant and
animal diversity is maintained. But even deeply entrenched ignorance about biodiversity will not keep a child from getting
into most professional schools, including some really good ones.
Indeed, he or she can do exceedingly well on either the LSAT
(Law School Admissions Test) or MCAT (Medical College Admissions Test) without even knowing the name *Darwin* or the
word *speciation*. So the existence of "evolution," the fact of "evolution," and the presence of hundreds if not thousands of "evolutionists" in our midst, including some occupying prestigious
chairs at prestigious universities, have virtually no effect on fundamentalist creationist children's ability to live in peace and earn
a decent wage.

It is one of the major mysteries of life that in a society as
complex, wealthy, and diverse as American society, one can be
blissfully ignorant of one of the truly major insights of all history and still be a successful doctor or lawyer. Maybe that fact
tells us more about complex societies than about anything else.
That fact is also a warning to the rational person. People blissfully ignorant of some of the most important intellectual accomplishments of all history (e.g., evolutionary theory) can and
do hold positions of major responsibility and power over the
lives of others. Ronald Reagan is a glaring example; history
books are filled with others, now sanitized by time and scholarship. It should not surprise anyone to discover how much of
that ignorance is excused in the name of religious belief.

The bottom line is, "evolution" does not make anyone a
criminal or one of society's pariahs. Poverty, abuse, bad role
models, desperation, drugs, perceived injustice, and easy money
contribute to the conditions that increase the chances of an individual becoming a pariah. Genetics also plays a part, although
an as yet largely un-agreed-upon part, in the production of in-

dividuals often treated as pariahs (homosexuals, obese, physically challenged, etc.), regardless of whether such individuals deserve that treatment or not, or even whether they behave as criminals or social misfits.

Theories of evolution have little to do with any social problems, with one notable exception, namely the evolution of social, political, and corporate structures. People do occasionally develop a rather cynical attitude about religion and sometimes become atheists or agnostics. Such people also may accept the assertions and observations of evolution, but that alone rarely makes one abandon the God concept. More likely, the corporate behavior of organized religion, the shallow and ill-concealed lust for power on the part of some of its practitioners, and broad knowledge of a variety of religions contributes more than evolution to a person's atheism or agnosticism. Broad knowledge about religion in general can be especially damaging to a rational and intelligent person's perceptions of Christianity. The more you know about the others, the less convinced you become that there is only one valid religion for all humanity. It is from such knowledge that skepticism develops.

Now a word about the politics of evolution, illustrated most clearly by those who try to force the teaching of creationism as an alternative explanation for the origin of life, particularly human life, in the schools. In today's public discourse, when we use the word *creationism*, we are referring primarily to a literal interpretation of the Biblical story of creation as found in the first part of Genesis. We are also referring to a deeper line of thought in which virtually all natural phenomena are interpreted as springing directly from God's hands, in accordance with God's plans, and ultimately vulnerable to God's judgment. Science, conversely, seeks natural, rather than supernatural, explanations for natural phenomena. One could easily accept the idea that God did indeed create the Universe and everything in it, but did so according to the methods revealed by modern science, i.e. Big Bang cosmology and post-Darwinian evolutionary biology. Evidently, to the creationists, this kind of merger between spiritualism and the discoveries of modern science is not an option.

Alternatively, one could easily argue that God created the universe with the Big Bang then walked away, or stepped back, or did whatever God does, and watched the scenario play itself out for several billion years. The net result of the scenario playing is the parade of life-forms that have occupied one planet in one galaxy. We don't know whether life exists elsewhere in the universe. We do know that a discussion of this possibility is a valid and interesting philosophical, as well as scientific, endeavor. What we also know is that during the early 1990s the United States Congress cut off funds for such explorations, as well as for other major research projects such as the supercollider to be built in northern Texas. The most myopic of these projects' critics cited the costs as justification for canceling the work. The most fearful probably paraded as myopic in order to hide their fear of the unknown. Many theorists predict, and I agree with this prediction, that discovery of intelligent life elsewhere in the universe would produce an immediate restructuring of Earth's religious politics.

But back to creation vs. evolution.

My simplistic view of the so-called creationist vs. evolutionist controversy is that it's not a controversy at all but rather a public display of (1) ignorance and abuse of powers derived from religion on the part of some Christian fundamentalists; (2) equal ignorance plus monumental gullibility on the part of these ministers' followers; and (3) a frightening capacity for humans in groups to be manipulated into believing almost anything, then acting on those beliefs. Even rational people may be uncomfortable with my characterization of some ministers as ignorant and abusive of their power. But think of the alternative characterization: they *know* that the modern scientific explanations for natural phenomena are legitimate, but *purposefully* teach the opposite, using the Bible as a vehicle for doing so. So it's most flattering to characterize such people as ignorant. Of course, many politicians can be most kindly so characterized, too.

As I've pointed out above, humans are free to believe anything, but they are not free to impose their beliefs on the secular affairs of society without opposition. This relationship between freedom of belief and restriction on action is a feature of natural law, especially as that law applies to humans (in the United States certain constitutional rights provide for expression of natural law). The same can be said for those whose beliefs are counter to the believers who are trying to force their beliefs on the former's secular affairs. Translation: it's okay to fight over creation vs. evolution. I'm doing it now. The creationists are wrong. God did not create the world in seven days and may not have created it at all. If God created the Earth we know, then He/She/It carried out that creation over a 4.5-billion-year period in which He/She/It allowed continents to drift and large numbers of micro-organisms, fungi, plants, and animals to evolve and become extinct and leave lots of fossils behind. And if He/She/It created the universe we know, then He/She/It probably carried out that creation with a Big Bang.

Quite frankly, although I'm more or less an agnostic, I do find the Big Bang a rather awesome idea, and the question of where the universe actually came from an equally awesome problem to ponder. That awe stems largely from knowledge of the universe and the planet Earth as revealed by modern science. But that same awe does not necessarily allow me to equate the God of the Big Bang with a God that warns an Adam not to eat of the Tree of Knowledge, then punishes him, casting a burden of original sin on all humankind, because he and Eve went ahead and ate of the Tree of Knowledge anyway and subsequently discovered his penis. That story is a beautiful and highly metaphorical one, but I don't believe for one minute that it's a literal one. God had the power to make Adam without a penis and cause all human births to be parthenogenetic (i.e., through the growth of unfertilized cells into embryos). God made plenty of other animals that reproduce this way. No, I don't think the God of the Big Bang would worry about Adam's penis. But I can see how the early Hebrews who either made up or picked up this creation myth might worry a lot about what kind of trouble humanity could get into with a penis.

The most common criticism directed at evolution by the creationists is that "it's only a theory." The creationists could add "but a falsifiable one," although they never do. To label a theory, or any of the hypotheses derived from that theory, as "falsifiable" is to pay that theory the supreme compliment, insofar as scientists are concerned (see chapter 5). Evolutionary theory is highly falsifiable; our vast knowledge of evolutionary events and processes derives from science's century and a half of attempting to falsify various evolutionary predictions. On the other hand, one has to study biology, geology, chemistry, and mathematics for many years in order to truly understand modern evolutionary theories and the research aimed at falsifying their predictions. Few creationists take the time and trouble to do this kind of study. For that matter, few citizens take the time and trouble, either, but many citizens feel qualified to argue about evolution vs. creation anyway.

The citizens that argue about creation vs. evolution also argue about virtually every other so-called controversy they encounter, for example Republican vs. Democrat solutions to social problems. A slightly higher proportion of these citizens study social issues than study evolution, but this study is not necessarily of the underlying statistics and original research, including methodology, that apply to the social problems they argue over (abortion, crime, economics, religion in the schools). More often than not, the general citizenry get its fodder for arguing about social problems from the same sources it gets its information for the evolution-creation argument, namely the newspapers, television, lobbyists, and like-minded friends. But to give them their due credit, citizens are better informed about social problems than they are about evolution for two reasons: first, the newspapers do a better job of educating the citizenry about social problems than they do with evolution, and second, social problems are easier to understand than science (or so we think).

The creationists don't need to restrict their "it's only a theory" criticism to evolution. They just as easily could say this about many theories, from quantum mechanics to strategic military planning. We have a multitude of theories, some of them broad, others more specific, some falsifiable (scientific), others clearly off-the-wall (nonscientific). My point is, "it's only a theory" is a criticism that could also be directed at the underlying tenets of Christianity (e.g., heaven, hell, and the existence of God). Furthermore, those theories (of heaven and hell) are unfalsifiable (i.e., nonscientific). They can never be "proven." They give rise to no falsifiable hypotheses about themselves. (They do give rise to scientific hypotheses about the *behavior of people who accept the untestable theories*, however; see chapter 5.) There are a great many theories that are "only theories" that we use for many purposes, such as building nuclear weapons and power plants.

So "it's only a theory" is a shallow criticism of evolutionary biology. My guess is that the creationists don't criticize many other (only) theories in this way because in so doing they would reveal themselves to be rather irrational. But there are some theories that merit a great deal of criticism as well as the detailed study this criticism would elicit. Strategic military planning involves many theories that might well fall into this category. For example, had the Domino Theory been as heavily criticized as Darwin's theories, we might never have entered the Vietnam war. The creationists lost an important opportunity to make the world a better place in which to live by not focusing their attention on the Domino Theory instead of the evolutionary one.

Although there is exceedingly strong evidence to support the idea that all organisms, from viruses to humans, evolve, there is absolutely unequivocal and incontrovertible evidence that some of our cultural entities evolve. A partial list of such entities includes: corporations, laws, societies, traditions, cultures, languages, ideas, technology, religion, art, music, war, and games. In most cases, the evolution of these entities follows a trajectory completely analogous to that postulated for most groups of organisms. That is, they have an origin and an institutional death (extinction); some species are replaced by related ones; some groups come to dominate their segment of society; some species give rise to numerous other species, and so forth. It is quite clear to any evolutionary biologist that extensive knowledge of the theories and examples of evolution would help any historian interpret the history of Western Christianity. Or, for that matter, the history of any government agency, corporation, or institution of higher learning.

In summary, every well-educated person knows that theories, observations, and interpretations of evolutionary biology do not threaten anyone's spirituality. These scientific products, however, do threaten the authority of those who use the Scriptures to maintain control over other humans. It all leads back to power, doesn't it? Ideas that erode an institution's power base are almost always rejected. And that principle is certainly not confined to the so-called evolution vs. creation controversy.

SEVEN

HETEROSEXUALITY

A nimals have been reproducing sexually for at least 600 million, and quite possibly as long as a billion, years. Many of their reproductive habits are bizarre beyond description. Some spiders have behaviors that would be considered Satanic if performed by humans. But the spiders act as if this kinky sex is perfectly normal; these creatures have been on earth for at least 300 million years. Scientists estimate that at any one time, there are a billion billion insects alive on earth. Virtually all insects reproduce sexually. Some of their mating rituals are also quite unusual. None of these billion billion insects crawls under sheets to perform sex (except maybe bedbugs), so not only are they out there doing it by the billions, they're doing it in public. "Bizarre" and "kinky" are value-laden human terms. We have no idea whether insects and spiders consider their sex normal. Insofar as we know, out of the millions of species that have occupied Earth, only one can't seem to understand that sex is a reasonably normal function. That one species, of course, is *Homo sapiens* (us).

There are about 5.7 billion people alive on Earth today. If we assume, just to give us some numbers to work with, that adult humans get laid at the rate of about once every three years, then approximately 100 million acts of human sexual intercourse occur every twenty-four-hour period. (As an aside, approximately 7 to 10 billion human defecations, 15 to 25 billion human urinations, and 3 to 7 billion human nose pickings also occur every 24 hours.) If this estimate is anywhere near correct, then there are nearly 40 billion acts of human sexual intercourse on Earth each year. We're still not up to the insects, by a very long shot, but 40 billion a year is a number well beyond the average citizen's capacity to visualize it. Even if the estimate is off by a factor of 10, there are still 4 billion such acts a year (or 400 billion, depending on whether the estimate is high or low by a factor of 10). But even if there are only 4 billion acts of human sexual intercourse each year, that number is too large for the average person to visualize. On a daily basis, the average person thinks in numbers far lower than a thousand. In essence, sex is so easily personalized in part because we have no way of understanding how common it is.

Of course it takes two people to perform a consensual sexual act. It's not clear whether we should count both partners' behavior as a separate sexual act, and if so, then the above figures should be doubled to 200 million every day. If you read Ann Landers, you discover that the typical adult American gets laid much more often than once every three years. If the typical European, Asian, African, and Indian is anything like the typical American, sexually speaking, then the above numbers might be increased by one, or even two, orders of magnitude.

Sticking with the once every three years figure, however (just to be on the conservative side), and referring to some of the popular sex literature available in any public library, then we must come to the conclusion that there must be a hell of a lot of masturbation going on between consensual acts with partners. It's not clear whether we should consider masturbation a heterosexual or homosexual act. Regardless of how one considers it, masturbation must be a remarkably common human behavior. Nonhuman primates also stimulate themselves, often in public in the zoos. If humans evolved from nonhuman primates, then humanoid animals have probably been masturbating for several million years, as a minimum. Although numerous sexual behavior studies have been published, often with much publicity (Kinsey; Masters and Johnson), I'll leave it to the individual reader to estimate, based on his or her personal experience, the amount of masturbation that occurs on Earth every 24 hours. My guess is that this estimate, like many other biological observations extended to the global population, is so high as to be shocking (or perhaps comforting?).

If sex in general is evil, and woman is the temptress, then the only conclusion we can draw from these reasonable estimates of human sexual activity is that Satan is with us everywhere all the time. On the other hand, most well-educated people consider consensual and solitary sex perfectly normal behaviors. Indeed, sex probably brings into focus more clearly than any other normal biological function the stranglehold Western Christianity has on humans by virtue of the "born in sin" idea.

The Catholic Church probably has as many strictures, pronouncements, and policies pertaining to private sexual behavior as any recorded system of religion, including some fairly pagan ones. The Catholics, of course, are famous for their fecundity, which suggests that Darwinian reproductive success can be influenced greatly by religion. But the Catholics are certainly not alone in their attention to sexual matters. Again I recommend consulting a local public library. There, among the books on sex, anthropology, psychology, and medicine, can be found an epic tale of humanity's monumental struggle with Satan, as exemplified by our efforts to regulate sex. Having digested the reference material, turn on the TV. Satan is winning.

However, many rational people think Satan is only a figment of the human imagination and therefore consider organized religion's preoccupation with sex to be a pathological joke. Sex itself is no joke; instead, it's probably the most personal, sensitive, vulnerable, and emotional behavior that humans regularly engage in. The main effect of religious interference with private human sexuality, however, is to remove this most sensitive and personal behavior from the realm of the personal and place it instead in the realm of government—in the very general sense of the word and in such organizations that have or seek power over large numbers of people, especially women. Male-dominated organized religion gains power, especially over women, by intruding into our most personal, sensitive, private, and emotional behavior—sex.

The reasons why organized religion has routinely considered women dangerous in the arena of sex are not very clear and are subject to much speculation. On the other hand, most organized religion is hierarchical, a decidedly male trait, and indeed most organized religions, especially the mainline American and Western Christian denominations, are predominantly male hierarchies. One only need flip channels on any local cable network to see several male preachers at work under the sponsorship of organized religion. One rarely if ever sees a woman in any of these roles, although Pat Robertson's cohost is an attractive lady who could not have been more skillfully cast. Pat Robertson, to his credit, does not use the pulpit as a power tool in the way some ministers with lesser quality body language do. Robertson's show is in a class by itself, when it comes to the use of television, combined with personal anecdote, to establish and maintain a powerful, religion-based organization. But the woman on Robertson's show has a decidedly subordinate job, namely that of confirming and validating the points of the two males. And neither of those two males would ever endorse consensual sex by a mature, well-educated, unmarried woman who knows perfectly well what she is doing.

Biological research suggests rather strongly that human males and females have different ways of organizing themselves into effective social units, given the chance to do so freely. Women tend to form cooperative groups; men tend to create dominance hierarchies. Dominance hierarchies spawn "leaders," subordinates, and mechanisms for advancing up the dominance scale, and they enable the participants to exercise a lot of power over both the environment and other human beings. In general, men are more interested in power than in sex. All of the traits that make a man a wonderful companion for a woman—sensitivity, gentleness, patience, tolerance, understanding, helpfulness, creativity—inhibit his success at operating inside a dominance hierarchy, especially one with a focus and a goal.

There is precious little in history books about women being able to divert male energies away from a drive to satisfy their thirst for power. There is much in the historical and current social record to suggest that *some* women are, instead, drawn to male power. And there is plenty of evidence that women who divert male energies away from power drives are considered dangerous. Nowhere in the Bible do we find particularly seductive males labeled as Satan. Such men must be a Hollywood product, having been absent in biblical times. Anyone who believes that should contact me immediately because I have some great bargain bridges for sale.

Sex is such a personal and emotional activity that it is highly vulnerable to intrusions of any kind. Western Christianity has recognized this vulnerability and managed repeatedly to intrude, wherever and whenever it suits the system, into the privacy of sex. When we combine this intrusion with the (unproven but at least somewhat likely) possibility that many women go to church in part to get away from their husbands for an hour or two, then we have a rather poisonous mixture. Maybe I'm stretching the point here, but there does exist a fair amount of "women's literature" that suggests church functions as a refuge at many levels and on many scales. In fact, in church, during church service and church functions, a woman is largely protected from sexual advances by her husband (although not necessarily from her minister or others in the congregation). If the popular literature has any truth to it, then marital relationships tend to be dynamic compromises often laced with suppressed hostility derived mostly from male dominance and its effects. In many cases, however, especially in the more conservative denominations, a woman who goes to church steps from one dominating relationship into another, and the second reaches all the way up to God. My Lutheran friends tell me, for instance, that a woman can't vote on church business. At home, however, at least in theory, she can cast the deciding vote on whether to have sex. I haven't checked this information for accuracy.

Televangelists give one the distinct impression that fundamentalist Christians find it quite disturbing to visualize even one act of sexual intercourse outside of a rigidly specified set of conditions. An example of such a disturbing sexual act would be one occurring between two unmarried but consenting people in their thirties. In fact, we have no idea who such people might be, only that their sexual union outside of marriage, ideally a happy, sharing, Christian marriage with a couple of well-adjusted Christian children, is fornication. It's fairly easy to find admonitions against fornication in the Bible (Matthew 15:18–20).

But it's also fairly easy to envision two unmarried, rational, well-educated, adult, healthy, professional, financially responsible people, quite attracted to one another, out on their fifth or sixth date, both agreeing that their attraction has quite a bit of potential for leading to something more serious. Being well educated, they've taken all the necessary precautions to avoid pregnancy and disease transmission, *just in case something happens.* As an exercise in rationality as it's applied to heterosexuality, try writing the conversation of these two people as they sit in a nice restaurant having a glass of wine about ten o'clock in the evening, after having been to a rather visually stimulating event at the Museum of Modern Art.

MALE: I'm very interested in sex with you. Are you interested?

FEMALE: Yes, I certainly am. But we're not married, and in Matthew, chapter 15, verses 18 through 20, it says fornication is a sin.

MALE: Sorry, I forgot. It must be the wine and those pictures. Whatever we do, I don't want to involve you in a sinful act.

FEMALE: I appreciate your courtesy and sensitivity. I'd hate to be kept out of heaven because we'd sinned on our sixth date.

MALE: You are a tower of strength. I've never met a woman like you. Will you marry me?

FEMALE: Certainly. Sex with you should be a lot of fun.

MALE: According to Jesus, you have already committed a sin by looking at me with a lustful eye. By all rights, you should tear your eye out.

FEMALE: Matthew 5:28 says nothing about women lusting after men, only men lusting after women.

MALE: Your biblical knowledge makes you even more attractive to me. [He takes a slow sip of his wine.] As a wife, of course.

FEMALE: Of course.

What's wrong with these conversations? Plenty. First, these characters' enslavement by the strictures of religion is completely inconsistent with their intelligence, education, values, perceptions, attitudes, and faith in their own, very human, capacity to make decisions that affect them personally. Secondly, they've been to one of the bastions of independent thinking, the Museum of Modern Art, which suggests they endorse personal freedom of expression and can't think of a single instance in which they've been harmed by a private act of painting performed in a studio. And finally, they're drinking wine and eating at a nice restaurant, both rather self-indulgent activities, and they're having a great time. The real issue here is that of personal choice vs. the dictates of someone else's interpretation of a religious document, not whether they should engage in a consensual sexual act. Sex is secondary; power over the individual's private life is the primary issue.

Let's assume these people do what they'd like to do, namely

join the rest of the 100 million humans who are going to get laid tonight. They are not hurting anyone if they crawl into the sack. They have some potential problems if she gets pregnant, but they're both prepared for such a possibility and are protecting themselves, and society, from an unwanted pregnancy (but not necessarily from a sexually transmitted disease). Their behavior is well within the norms of human behavior since recorded history began. No one is going to get shot because of their consensual sexual act, no illegal drugs are going to be sold, no child pornography or abuse will result from this act, no wars will be declared, no one will eliminate 10,000 jobs from a manufacturing plant because of their roll in the hay, no famine will descend on a Third World nation as a result of their evening's culmination.

Now substitute some secular authority for the religious authority in the above conversation.

MALE: Interested in sex?
FEMALE: Yeah, but section 7b of City Ordinance 367A says we have to wait until we get married.
MALE: Thanks for reminding me. I'd hate to involve you in a misdemeanor on just our sixth date.

If your local library is anything at all like mine, it contains a world of nonfiction literature that describes societies in which religion combines with secular authority to a degree implied by the above conversation.

Criminal laws, tend to focus on nonconsensual sex acts (rape), acts in which one of the individuals is legally unfranchised (sexual child abuse, statutory rape), acts in which violence occurs (assault, murder, use of a weapon), and so on. Adultery, one of the biblical anathemas, is usually covered by civil, rather than criminal, laws (e.g., as grounds for divorce as opposed to grounds for arrest, indictment, trial, conviction, and imprisonment). Prostitution is typically dealt with in a sort of in-limbo fashion, often being technically illegal but sometimes difficult

to investigate and expensive to prosecute. Prostitution tradi-
tionally has a number of secondary effects, however, which are
detrimental to society. But prostitution is not called "the old-
est profession" for nothing. Reading the daily newspapers, I get
the distinct feeling that organized religion has given up on prostitution in deference to the fertile grounds for outrage afforded
by the increasingly visible lifestyle of homosexuals.

Protestant fundamentalism also has little to say about the entire spectrum of sexual harassment, deferential treatment, and
governmental actions based on gender that pervade American
(and certainly other) society. I'm speaking here of everything
from early childhood emphasis on certain educational tracks
(technical and financial for the boys, artistic and domestic for
the girls) to society's worship of male athletic heroes and the
print media's preoccupation with male corporate heads and
middle management; war as the ultimate trump card in politics
(as opposed to negotiated cooperative settlements); the narrative structure of everything from sitcoms to commercials; and
the rather extraordinary level of sexism in the military forces.
Thus our society considers it perfectly acceptable for organized
religion, often operating through the parents, to tell a brilliant
six-year-old girl that the world began in 4004 when God created the universe in seven days, that evolution is "just a theory,"
that the proper place for a girl is either at home taking care of
her husband's children or working at some caring profession
(nurse and physical therapist are okay), and that home schooling is superior to public schooling because you can't pray in the
public schools. My assertion is that such behavior on the part
of organized religion is a form of abuse, intellectual abuse, that
is just as detrimental to society as other forms of gender-specific
activity. Of course there are no laws against lying to and ma-
nipulating children, male or female, under the stern rubric of
religion.

If Satan is among us, he is certainly operating in subtle as
well as overt ways. And his more subtle schemes—for instance,
that of providing females with the same educational and pro-

fessional opportunities as males and, in fact, encouraging females to seek the same educational and professional opportunities—look suspiciously like behaviors that erode and threaten the male dominance hierarchy of fundamentalist Western Christianity.

EIGHT

HOMOSEXUALITY

Fundamentalist Christianity generally considers homosexuality one of the most repulsive, repugnant, despised, evil, sinful, despicable, deviant, un-Christian phenomena known to humankind. Homophobia, however, has an added, rather biological, component that I'll call "the Other." "The Other" is a rather well recognized psycho-social phenomenon manifested in all forms of human biology, from allergic reactions to racism. Any person who is not like us is "the Other." In effect, defining a person, or a group of persons, as "the Other" is tantamount to depriving that person, or group, of membership in the human race (see E. O. Wilson's *On Human Nature*). Such deprivation is a prelude to murder and war, as well as to other, lesser, forms of abuse.

Although it has nothing to do with homosexuality, the most dramatic recent demonstration of the use of "the Other" as a prelude to destruction was United States president George Bush's political manipulation of the American public prior to the Persian Gulf War. For this reason, the case is worthy of study before we get to the homosexual as "the Other." All rational people understand clearly that the Persian Gulf War could just as easily have been called the Christian Energy War.

There is no doubt that Saddam Hussein is a very unsavory character. Like many administrations throughout history, his is guilty of massive human rights violations and acts that make it more difficult, not easier, for Iraqi citizens to live safe, healthy lives. One of those acts was to invade his neighboring country of Kuwait. Of course Saddam had been trying for eight years to invade another of his neighbors, Iran, but that particular attempt did not inspire an American bombing raid on Baghdad.

I'm not defending Saddam Hussein or trying to excuse anything he may have done to contribute to the eventual war. Nor am I criticizing American military personnel under contract obligation to do the job of soldiering. But for nearly six months after the Iraqi invasion of Kuwait, George Bush painted Saddam Hussein with a Satanic brush. A careful review of all Bush's public pronouncements on the subject of the Iraqi invasion reveals a constant and almost primeval litany of evil, nonhuman behavior, attributed to Saddam. Bush's verbalizations on the subject of Iraq could have been written by any anthropology doctoral student in response to a written comprehensive question: What does a person in a position of power do in order to get his subjects to gladly kill other human beings? The answer, of course, is to dehumanize the victims. In Bush's case, the technique worked like a charm.

Fundamentalist Western Christianity is working overtime to characterize homosexuals as the Other. It's difficult to determine exactly what will be accomplished when this goal is achieved. Whether the religious right intends it or not, one of the products of homosexual's dehumanization is increased violence and decreased efforts, on the part of elected public law enforcement officials, to stop such violence. If allowed to proceed, this kind of social evolution can lead to relatively extreme oppression and discrimination against people known to behave, in private, in certain ways related to sex. Recent attempts to revoke laws protecting homosexuals from discrimination (e.g. in Colorado) are an illustration of social and cultural evolution toward legalized dehumanization of humans on the basis of their private sexual behavior. (The Colorado Supreme Court reversed the voter-approved initiatives.)

Taken as a whole, all commonly available information on homosexuality suggests the following:

1. There is no way to predict whether a child will be a homosexual or not. Christian parents, as well as non-Christian parents, unmarried parents, rich parents, poor parents, parents in any part of the world, are all equally likely to produce a homosexual child.

2. The vast majority of homosexuals who have spoken publicly on the subject indicate that they "knew they were different" from a very early age, certainly no later than puberty.

3. Homosexual behavior is culturally and socially pervasive, but at a relatively constant and relatively low level. That is, it occurs among all walks of life, all occupations, all economic classes, all ethnic and racial categories, all geographic regions. Homosexuals claim that on the average, about 10% of the people you meet are gay; some studies of American sexual behavior indicates the fraction of homosexuals in the American population is closer to 1%.

4. Homosexuality does not appear to be associated with any particular criminal behavior, although these statistics are not easy to get and confirm. If homosexuality is a willful sin, as opposed to a phenomenon influenced largely by genetics, then it should be statistically associated with other willful evil behavior. Nothing we see in the media indicates this relationship has been established.

5. If homosexuality is a sinful lifestyle choice, then it should manifest itself as a rebellious behavior among youth. That expectation is not met. If all

the available literature is correct, then homosexual behavior among young people is a source of extreme personal stress and self-questioning. Drinking, smoking, skipping school, doing drugs, having babies, and fighting, on the other hand, are all fairly common forms of rebellious youthful behavior that are socially damaging lifestyle choices.

6. There is an ongoing debate among scientists, social scientists, and physicians over the extent to which homosexuality is genetically determined or influenced. As with most human behaviors, the genetic influences are extremely difficult to separate out from the cultural influences. What the social scientists have consistently failed to do, however, is associate homosexuality with certain parenting techniques or other regularly occurring patterns of childhood experience.

Although this book is not the place to present such a discussion, there is plenty of evidence that certain forms of adult behavior *are* strongly influenced by childhood experiences, and that not all these behaviors are socially beneficial. Good illustrations of such instances include brilliant women directed into housewifing or low-paying careers as a result of religious upbringing (extraordinarily common) or pathologically insecure men ending up as middle managers (also reasonably common).

7. The issue of homosexual "lifestyle choice" as a public health hazard is basically an irrational and political one created and maintained by the religious and political right. Granted, there is compelling evidence that many of the original AIDS cases in the United States can be traced to a single homosexual male (see Shilts's *And the Band*

Played On). There is equally compelling evidence that the Reagan administration increased the public health hazards of AIDS, during the 1980s, by choosing to consider HIV infection a problem only for homosexuals.

In fact, the public burden of "unhealthy lifestyle choice" is a massive one but so far, at least in the United States, very little of that burden is due to homosexuality or AIDS. Most of the burden results from cardiovascular disease, the incidence of which is strongly influenced by "lifestyle choice" (diet, lack of exercise, smoking). Second in line is cancer, also strongly influenced by "lifestyle choice" (living near radiation sources, alcohol abuse, exposure to certain chemicals, smoking). I don't know where production agriculture falls on the list of public health hazards, but farming and ranching are exceedingly hazardous occupations. And driving an automobile—another obvious "lifestyle choice"—kills at least 30,000 people a year and maims many more than that.

If there is a significant public health danger from sexually transmitted AIDS, it's far more likely to result from good-ole-boy type heterosexual behavior than from homosexual acts between consenting adults. Indeed, the global prostitution trade has all the potential for producing an explosion of AIDS cases (see *Time* magazine, June 21, 1993), which many will interpret as the arrival of the Fourth Horseman of the Apocalypse. Metaphorically, such interpretation is correct. Metaphorically. In my view, the political and religious right ought to be far more worried about slavery and prostitution than about homosexuality.

In summary, there is little evidence to suggest that homosexuality *per se* is Satan's work and plenty to suggest that homosexuality, like many forms of sexual behavior, is anathema to people who lead with the phrase "I'm a Christian . . ." Most homosexuals are committing only the sin of being different. I say "only." The "sin" of being different is at the heart of many of humanity's most beastly moments, from the Holocaust to the seething bitter violence in the Balkans to the malignant racism and ethnocentrism we see every day throughout the world.

Rational people let other human beings be themselves until "being themselves" generates a clear and present danger. So far, regardless of how traumatic homosexuality has been for anyone personally, and for whatever reason, there is little evidence that any *society* is in danger from private consensual hetero- or homosexual acts between adults. Homosexual acts involving nonconsenting minors fall into the same categories of criminal behavior that govern other kinds of assault and abuse (including nonconsensual heterosexual acts). The historical record on homosexuality as a *relative* danger to society is fairly clear: War (political lifestyle choice), fiscal irresponsibility (political lifestyle choice), environmental deterioration (political and economic lifestyle choice), and the drug trade (difficult to characterize in terms of fundamental nature) are all significantly greater public health hazards, especially in the long term, than consensual homosexuality. It's time for this nation to start worrying about some bigger problems than adult sexual preferences and predispositions.

NINE

RACISM

Race is a factor in all transactions between people of different ethnic backgrounds. It matters not what the races are—Asian vs. Indian, Indian vs. African, Asian vs. Caucasian, Caucasian vs. African—race is a factor in transactions even as simple as saying hello. In this regard, racism is as deeply embedded in the human psyche as sexism. Truly educated people understand clearly how instinctively they react to people of other races, and thus they use this understanding to defuse racial tensions whenever possible.

There are some who argue that racism is not necessarily the work of Satan. After all, the Bible is filled with tribes that considered themselves God's Chosen People and considered everyone else worthy of destruction. The world is still filled with such tribes, although now the tribes call themselves nations. A quick reading of any weekly news magazine reveals that much of the current global conflict is based on racism, religion, and cultural differences among nations and populations. Rarely do people of the same culture fight one another when they could be fighting people of a different culture.

Is racism a work of Satan? That is such a difficult question to answer that we find ourselves wondering whether Satan actually works to make issues convoluted and self-contradictory, rather than simply doing evil things like impregnating unsuspecting women. If so, then Satan is much more cunning, intelligent, and well educated than we suspect. Of course those who are willing to attribute all of the world's evils to Satan are also willing to give him any set of traits necessary to perpetuate that evil. But one has to be pretty sophisticated to understand why it's a Satanic act to make an issue convoluted, self-contradictory, and paradoxical. Here's the explanation: problems with a biological basis are virtually impossible to solve. Racism is such a problem; it can't be solved on a population level, but it can be controlled and legally discouraged. Indeed, racism eventually will rip apart any society that fails to control it.

Rejection of nonself is pervasive in the animal kingdom and has a molecular basis in humans in the form of the immune system. When we get hay fever, our bodies are rejecting nonself (in this case, pollen). When we get a vaccination, say, against measles, then the doctor is increasing the speed and specificity with which we reject nonself (the measles virus). If we reject nonself (the measles virus) quickly and effectively enough, then we will not get the disease called measles. In an analogous manner, if we reject any kind of cultural and ethnic nonself quickly and effectively enough, we will not get the "diseases" called tolerance and understanding. So in dealing with racism, we're up against a formidable problem that is deeply intertwined among our genes. Fortunately, although such problems can rarely if ever be solved, they can be controlled by patience, tolerance, understanding, education, and efforts to behave ethically.

The first step in controlling this problem of racism is learning to appreciate the lessons of statistics, the rules of probability, and the principles of genetics. I have done my homework on this matter. Anyone is welcome to refute the following assertion with any kind of a study: among any 300 healthy newborn babies selected at random, regardless of race, one will find almost the full range of intellectual potential represented in the human species as a whole. Granted, there may not be any

Mozarts or Einsteins, but those two are so far beyond the norms as to be statistically quite unlikely even if you select at random a million, or even 5 million, healthy newborn babies. I'm completely convinced that out of any 300, however, will be rocket scientists, molecular biologists, powerful artists and writers, responsible and loving future mothers and fathers, people perfectly qualified to be presidents of major universities and nations, as well as a few misfits.

The key words in the above paragraph, of course, are "random" and "healthy." Healthy babies are a blessing, but the health of the mother does not guarantee, only increases the probability of, a healthy baby. Conversely, certain kinds of unhealthy practices of mothers are known to increase the likelihood that a baby will be born unhealthy. Narcotics and alcohol use, HIV infection, and lack of proper diet are all factors that reduce the health of a mother and increase the chances a baby will be born unhealthy.

It is a common perception that unhealthy mothers are not randomly distributed among the American population, and that as a consequence, the chances of being born unhealthy are greater for some ethnic categories, and some socio-economic classes, than for others. If true, this nonrandom distribution alone guarantees that babies born to those mothers will not necessarily be representative of healthy babies considered at random, that is, they will not necessarily fall within the 300 babies mentioned above. So maternal health and proper diet are rather fundamental factors in allowing our statistics to apply. The first task a nation faces in dealing with the destructive long-term consequences of racism is to ensure, insofar as possible, that *all* its babies are born healthy, regardless of ethnic or racial background.

This matter of the human potential for newborn healthy babies selected at random without regard for race is at the heart of the racism problem. As soon as one understands this aspect of human biology, racism is suddenly seen as highly destructive for all concerned, not just the minority members of our society. It's quite simple: any purely social factor that withdraws human intellectual potential from the supply upon which our nation depends is a social factor that is destructive to our national integrity. Any purely social factor that operates to divert intellectual potential into criminal behavior multiplies that destructiveness.

Translated into pure and simple terms: an investment in health care, education, safety, equal opportunity, and the provision of positive role models, all regardless of race, is a necessary investment in the economic and social health of a nation. It is impossible to eliminate evil by such an investment. It is possible to reduce that evil to such a level that the American dream remains alive, and the American experiment in human dignity and freedom continues. If this conclusion sounds like liberal utopian idealism, then so be it. The issue is not whether I am correct, which I am, but whether this basically statistical and neutral view of our society and its human resources guides our national policies, which of course it does not.

One aspect of racism that is not widely appreciated is that the laws of genetics, probability, and chance operate just as inexorably at the personal level as they do at the population level. *We have no control whatsoever over how we are born!* Our parents had plenty of control over who we grew up to be, but we have no control whatsoever over who our parents are. We have the power to thank our lucky stars that we were not born of a certain genetic makeup, but 5.7 billion other people on this planet also have the power to thank *their* lucky stars that they were not born into *our* circumstances with *our* genes. I don't care how a person looks, where that person lives, how much money he or she has, *somebody* on Earth thinks that individual is scum and is revulsed by the very thought of possibly having been born into the other's body at this time in history. Alternatively, some may wish they were born someone else. But they weren't. And they're never going to be. We have no choice but to make peace with the genes we have. In this regard we are the equal of the person we hate because of his or her race.

I heartily recommend E. O. Wilson's book *On Human Nature*, listed in the appendix, as reading material to begin a program of self-education on the matter of racism. What Wilson tells us is that humans have certain inborn behaviors but that culture strongly shapes them. Thus the *fact* of a behavior is of genetic origin, but the *form* of that behavior is of cultural origin. For example, we are going to carry out aggression. But our choice of weapons—hydrogen bombs, words, religion, movies, or money—is a cultural phenomenon. It is clear from Wilson's book, based on decades of serious and widely recognized scientific scholarship, that we will exhibit racism, period. The manner in which we manifest that racism, however, is something we learn. We learn to accept people for what they are and we learn to help others achieve their highest potential because such achievement helps maintain our common, relatively rich society. Some of us also learn to hate others simply because those others do not match our perception of what a human being should be. This last kind of learning is dangerous to everyone.

One of Wilson's more enlightening discussions is found in the chapter on aggression. There we find, laid out in eloquent terms, what every anthropologist knows, namely that (1) we define humanity by our language; (2) we are perfectly capable of "eliminating" other humans, societies, and cultures from membership in the human species simply by talking about them in certain ways; and (3) denial of membership in the human species is a prelude to violence. We do all three of these behaviors almost instinctively, and cultural forces can enhance greatly our tendency to do them.

For example, a large fraction of the American public does not act as if it believes Arabs in general, and Muslims in particular, belong to the human race. On the other hand, to most Americans, Jews are founding members of the species. All of the Old Testament, more correctly referred to as the Hebrew Bible, is Jewish "history." Many of our most basic and cherished moral codes and beliefs have a Hebrew origin, and the most notable of our wars (WWII) had a strong Righteous Us vs. Evil Them component, the evil being Hitler and his Holocaust. American financial health is inextricably intertwined with that of the Jewish minority. Many of our most successful and beloved comedians, our most successful writers, are Jewish. We have no such historical, cultural, and intellectual relationships with the Arabs, regardless of their having kept science—upon which our culture now firmly rests—alive during the Dark Ages. To Americans, especially younger ones, Arabs equate with oil, not with the Ten Commandments. But what Americans, especially the younger ones, tend to forget is that current American prosperity and standard of living depend largely on Arab oil.

When I bring up the subject of Arabs, the vast majority of my successful doctor and lawyer friends will immediately start talking about oil and Saddam Hussein. However, if one of them is truly educated, he or she will start talking about Yasir Arafat and the uneasy peace agreements negotiated between Israel and the Palestine Liberation Organization during 1993. And, if one of these people has spent time in the Middle East, he or she may spin a wondrous tale of rich Arabic cultural traditions, powerful spirituality, and a lively people who've made their adjustments to life in an ecologically harsh environment. Of course that person might also talk about the not-so-enlightened aspects of life in the Middle East, especially if that person is female. But an Arab who'd spent time in the United States could, in much the same manner, go home and talk about gang warfare in South Central Los Angeles instead of the wonders of a free press as revealed by the Watergate incident.

This digression about Arabs and Jews is intended to illustrate the way in which our language and culture predispose us to treat others as if they belong, or do not belong, to the human species. In its most pernicious form, racism and ethnocentrism use language to deny people membership in the species, such denial being a prelude to, if not outright justification for, other acts that reinforce the perceived nonhuman status of the target race or ethnic group. Typical acts against those considered less than human, acts firmly recorded in American history, include murder, political oppression, slavery, as well as an enormous number and variety of lesser affronts, insults, and discriminations. History is clear on one point: All of these events are to be expected when different ethnic groups encounter one another. Prejudice is not a uniquely American problem. But history is equally clear on an additional point, although that point is not nearly so widely acknowledged: Such violent and discriminatory racial and ethnic interactions are not to the long-term benefits of any modern society that practices them.

In terms of percentages (although not necessarily in terms of absolute numbers), violence and crime have a disproportionate impact on the black community. Black Americans are much more likely than whites, especially in the case of males, to end up in prison. In general, black Americans who enter the criminal justice system often get harsher sentences than their white American counterparts. In terms of absolute numbers, however, there are many more white drug users than black, many more whites on welfare than blacks, and there is a great deal of murder, armed robbery, and rape committed by whites in the United States against other whites.

Virtually all scholarly studies that have been done equate increased levels of violent crime with decreased levels of education, family integrity, and opportunities for meaningful employment. So what are we to do about the problems of unequal distributions of social and cultural opportunities, unequal distributions of crime and punishment, unequal distributions of membership in the human species? This is an extraordinarily difficult question to answer. Generations of political and religious leaders have failed to answer it. Furthermore, it's not obvious from a study of anthropology and history that any solutions are likely to be permanent.

Our personal and individual cultural experiences are so deep, so all-consuming, that it requires substantial effort on the part of a single human being to override his or her initial reaction to people of a different race or ethnic group. Tolerance of nonself is one of the most fragile of human traits. Stereotyping— of other cultures—is perhaps the most important factor that prevents us from solving problems of prejudice. Indeed, such stereotyping is indispensable to sustained military conflict (see Paul Fussell's *Wartime*). Virtually all races stereotype other races, and the stereotypes are found throughout art, poetry, literature, and music, that is, throughout the elements that bind a culture together. It is probably naive and idealistic on my part to suggest that the most effective battle an individual can fight against the socially destructive forces of racism is the battle against stereotypes.

Multiculturalism is a word that describes society's formal efforts to reduce our tendency to stereotype others. We now have multicultural programs, teachers, curricula, and library materials to match the cultural diversity that has characterized our athletic teams and armies for the past generation. I am not promoting a liberal social agenda when I say that these efforts should be supported to some extent. Education and encounter are proven mechanisms for reducing racial tensions. The education tends to maximize the strengths of all, dispel myths, and spread economic benefits through access to employment. Encounter, especially of a positive kind, helps erode the nonself rejection tendency and often provides a firsthand demonstration that stereotypes do not apply. But at some point in this educational process, the inherent divisiveness of multiculturalism must give way to the realization that we all live together on, and ultimately depend on, the only planet in the universe known to support life, and that we get along best when we speak the same language.

Trying to build a generation of tolerance from the start is one of the few things anyone can do locally and immediately to make the world a better place in which to live. Actively become tolerant and understanding of difference, if no place else than in the privacy of your own home. Listen to music, read literature, and watch television programs that are culturally diverse. Let's get over our fear of "the Other." "The Same" has more potential for disrupting our lives than does "the Other," simply because "the Same" has a lot of power to convince us that war against "the Other" is in our best interest, if not downright essential to maintain the utopian dream. Nothing could be further from the truth.

TEN

THE PUBLIC SCHOOLS

THE TREE OF KNOWLEDGE

In the second chapter of Genesis, God says to Adam: *From any tree of the garden you may eat freely; but from the Tree of Knowledge of good and evil you shall not eat, for in the day that you eat from it you shall surely die.* This one passage must be either the most profound or the most shallow of any in the Bible. The profundity is to be found in its (apparent) foresight, and in its applicability, in retrospect, to the mountains of knowledge science has delivered on the subject of human behavior and origins. The shallowness is in its self-contradiction and in the rather sexist text that follows Adam and Eve's sampling of the tree. Nevertheless, a good many believe that the public schools, our formal system for eating of the Tree of Knowledge of good and evil, are the work of Satan. Today we have Pat Robertson declaring that the public schools should be closed. For some idiotic reason, people still send him money.

A rational study of public education demands that we examine both the shallowness of God's warning as well as its profundity. Humanism is at the center of this discussion because public education is our major mechanism for answering the question What should I do with my life on Earth? The first,

most pervasive, most time-consuming answer, and one that oc-
cupies much of an American's formative years, is *go to school.*
Throughout all of our modern history, education has been seen
as central to whatever else we accomplish. Public education
concerns earthly, secular matters, at least of late, and especially
secular matters such as voting intelligently, making a living,
obeying laws of the land, reading, and controlling technology.
Public schools fail most often when we allow them to become
mainly places where children develop athletic prowess and find
mates.

The alternative to original sin would have been for Eve to
resist the snake, avoid the Tree of Knowledge, and for all of her
and Adam's descendents to similarly avoid eating of the Tree
of Knowledge. In such a scenario, we'd probably all still be living in the Garden of Eden, eating sweet fruits and reproducing without knowing what we were doing or covering our private parts. Would we be better off, and more of a satisfaction
to God, if we didn't have to vote intelligently, make a living,
and control technology? That's a good but unanswerable question. Actually we'd be living a lot like chimpanzees. Insofar as
I can tell, both chimpanzees and gorillas live very much like
Adam and Eve did prior to the Fall. Chimpanzees and gorillas
don't seem to have quite the same kinds of problems that we
do, but who's to say they don't also have problems that to them
seem particularly enigmatic? For example, chimps might be
constantly asking, in their own way, What should I do with my
life on Earth?

Chimpanzees and gorillas present us with a difficult problem in the analysis of secular education as a Satanic phenomenon. The problem is this: *Chimpanzees and gorillas must learn how
to get along in their gardens of Eden.* They must acquire the skills
of tool-making, learn how to be a parent, learn to recognize the
individuals in their bands, and figure out how to move up the
dominance hierarchy. Even though they live in gardens of Eden,
chimps and gorillas still have their own brand of secular responsibilities and problems to solve.

SELF-CONTRADICTION

Perhaps if we examine the self-contradictory nature of God's warning first, then the profundity will offer some saving grace to what seems on the surface like a rather blasphemous discussion. I contend that the warning of Genesis—not to eat of the Tree of Knowledge of good and evil—is an extraordinarily capricious and self-contradictory command, indeed, a rather un-Godly one. When I say "un-Godly," I'm speaking of God of the Big Bang, the God that made the universe. Capriciousness and self-contradiction are so human a pair of traits, that one must truly wonder whether God would behave in such a way. Such wonder relies, however, on a fairly extensive knowledge of the universe. Anyone who knows anything at all about the universe as revealed by modern science can see immediately that the self-contradiction and capriciousness of this warning are exceedingly un-Godlike and equally exceedingly humanlike. A God made by humans in a *human* image, however, might well behave in a capricious and self-contradictory way.

The theological self-contradiction lies in the "of good and evil" portion of the warning. Presumably, one of the major functions of religion is moral guidance. The most elemental factor of moral behavior is the ability to distinguish between good and evil. If we give maximum credit to all those individuals, both real and fictitious, who labor throughout the Bible to teach us the difference between good and evil and who constantly search for ways to do (their perceptions of) God's will, then we must conclude that knowledge of good and evil is most elementary to our success at behaving like a rational person, a goal easily attainable by one who generally considers himself/herself a Christian (I don't know enough about other religions to comment on them in this regard). If we distance ourselves from knowledge of good and evil, then we have no way of distinguishing between the two.

Is God hinting that if we don't know the difference between good and evil then it doesn't matter which we do? I doubt it. I contend that the "God" of Genesis is really talking about non-sex and sex when he talks about good and evil, respectively. One of the more revealing factors in this warning is its context, especially in the conversations and qualifiers that surround Eve's disobeyance. Suddenly the Fall begins to look suspiciously like just one more ancient expression of an overriding sexism and fear of women. First of all, there's nothing in Genesis that indicates God told Eve directly about the tree. In fact, in chapter 2, God issues the warning before He issues Eve; she's not even alive and present so we must presume God expects Adam to tell Eve, as well as control her behavior.

Secondly, Eve hasn't gotten the whole story straight, a situation familiar to all public school teachers. She admits to the snake that they must not eat of the tree, but she calls it the "tree in the middle of the garden" instead of the "Tree of Knowledge of good and evil." Any public school teacher knows that a tree of knowledge of good and evil is a much more significant tree than one in the middle of a garden. Adam may have told Eve not to eat off the tree in the middle of the garden but he didn't engage her in much of an intellectual discussion or a review of the rationale behind his edict. He treated her like a bimbo and paid the price, so to speak, perhaps the first, but certainly not the last, such instance in the history of human affairs.

But the most revealing aspect of this tale is what Adam and Eve do with their knowledge: They discover their genitals and sew together loincloths out of leaves in order to cover themselves up. With verse 7, chapter 2, the writers of Genesis focus our attention on sex, particularly sex as an expression of evil, sex as something that cannot be controlled, sex as a curse of woman that she constantly tries to share with man, and sex as a source of pain. In all honesty, we must conclude that if the Genesis myths have any basis in prehistory, then sex and the pain of childbirth must have been as much of a problem for Neanderthal and Cro-Magnon people as for today's teenagers.

Adding to the capriciousness of the Fall tale is God's handling of the discovered transgression. Instead of saying to Adam,

"You incompetent, weak fool, I put you in charge but you let someone else talk you into disobeying my most important command!" God says to Eve, "What is this you have done?" God then sets the tone for the rest of organized religion's domination of women and distaste for sex by increasing her groaning, including the labor of childbirth (surely well known by Neanderthals and Cro-Magnons), making her husband her master, and strangely enough, also making her "eager for your husband." If I didn't know better, I'd consider Genesis, chapter 2, to be the story line source for many of television's most objectionable programs (e.g., daytime soaps).

At this point, I presume, sex was defined as punishment and thus no longer became fun. The Southern Baptist Convention could not have devised a more effective means of incorporating sex into the arsenal of weapons with which it fights the war on normal human behavior. This pervasive Christian theme of sexual pleasure as sin lies behind much of organized religion's opposition to sex education in the public schools. Ideally, such education would slow the transmission of Human Immunodeficiency Virus (HIV), and the fatal disease it causes, as well as reduce the number of unwanted pregnancies by teenage unmarried women.

"Knowledge" as Technology

I suppose literalists could argue that God is omnipotent, therefore any properties, desires, and actions we attribute to God are not only plausible but in fact true. Following this line of "logic," literalists might say that the omnipotent God *really did* mean 20th-century technology when he warned of "knowledge." Any reasonably well educated rational person knows that 20th-century technology is only the latest stage in a long history of technological advance. Humans, and possibly even prehumans, have been using technology to make one another miserable for centuries if not millennia, beginning, likely, with unshaped

stones and large animal leg bones used as weapons. Certainly
fire, the long bow, the sword, the rifle, and the cannon have
all taken their toll of human life. Certainly the advent of the
printing press, sextant, telescope, microscope, and sailing ship
were as disruptive of human society in their day as television
is now. Even chimpanzees make tools and use them (e.g., long
stripped twigs for extracting termites from their mounds). Efforts of human researchers to duplicate this rather routine
chimpanzee behavior reveal that the making and use of termite
twigs are highly sophisticated skills that humans do not acquire
easily. I learned this from watching the Discovery channel on
cable TV. If God meant "technology" when He said "knowledge," he could as easily have been talking about chimps as people.

After the transgression, God the Omnipotent, from having
already made chimpanzees and gorillas and watched them operate in the Garden of Eden, could, and probably should, have
said to Adam and Eve, Where did you learn how to make
weapons? Where did you learn how to dig up parts of my Garden in order to selectively grow others? Where did you learn
how to divert my favorite stream to irrigate your vegetable
patch? Where did you learn how to imitate the whistles of certain birds in order to draw them close enough to kill? Have you
been eating of the Tree of Knowledge? Then Adam and Eve
would likely have said yes, we ate of the Tree of Knowledge and
learned the technology to make our lives easier. Then God the
Omnipotent could have said, Well, it was probably inevitable,
given that you were made only in my image and not an exact
replicate; but let me tell you this, Adam and Eve, tools can cut
people, including your children, as easily as they can cut your
food, and unless your descendents learn to use their tools wisely,
they will eventually destroy themselves. That would have been
a profound conversation on God's part—wisdom worthy of in-
clusion in secular school curricula.

Instead, God says, "Who told you that you were naked?"
Nakedness has been a problem for Christians ever since.

Not long ago I had an opportunity to talk to a staff member in one of the nation's premier art museums, one that hosts guided tours for thousands of public school children each year.

"We've started getting calls," this person told me, "from the religious conservatives wanting us to make sure their children don't see any nudes. They even wanted us to cover up certain paintings when their children's school came to visit."

"So what happened when those kids showed up?"

"The little boys wanted to know where the naked ladies were," the staff member replied.

Those who despair over the plight of the public schools take note: Some things get these kids' attention and hold it. My advice: Start a subversive all-out campaign against math, science, and good literature. Make them hidden and forbidden subjects and include them in the original sin, then maybe the little boys will find them as attractive as the naked ladies. Come to think of it, from what I read in the newspapers and hear on Pat Robertson's television show, that's already being tried and it doesn't work to stimulate interest in math, science, and literature. From what my college teacher sources tell me, children from the religious right come to college afraid of math, science, and good literature and not nearly so eager to find them as they are to find naked ladies.

In essence, then, Creation and the Fall are wonderful myths, colorful, elegant, and with a certain lyrical literary quality to them. But they are still only myths. The God of Genesis is a god who is worried most about knowledge of sex and punishes the transgressors by making women subservient to their husbands and making the consequences of sex (in this case, childbirth) painful. The God of Genesis is not the profound God of Foresight. Through *our* interpretations of the Fall, we are able to make the fairy tale consistent with our current experience. The profundity of this Tree of Knowledge story is, itself, a human construction. Here we have the strength, indeed the truth, of the Bible, namely its broad applicability, which becomes available through our very human acts of interpretation.

PROFUNDITY

When I interpret God's warning as profundity, that interpretation is based on acquired knowledge of science and technology. The warning is a forward echo of what every practicing scientist and engineer knows from eating of the Forbidden Tree, namely that science and technology are distinctly two-edged swords. Thus whenever we use these swords to cut a problem, a sharp edge is always facing backward, toward us. This description of science and technology is a metaphorical, or symbolic, one. Its application is very tangible, however, and in any library many examples can be found of science and technology having backfired on their owners. In virtually all of these cases, "ownership" has passed from the individual scientist to the public prior to the backfire. And in such cases, said reversal comes when politicians seek to use science and technology for economic and political gain. That is, when politicians think that they can turn a sharp edge toward their enemies without having an equally sharp edge facing backward, then everyone gets cut. If there is one history lesson worth learning, it's that politicians are generally pretty naive when it comes to science and technology.

The only knowledge that is truly dangerous to all humanity, in the biblical sense of God's warning, is that of science and technology. Knowledge of arts and crafts, music, history, literature, and religion is not dangerous. It is, instead, uplifting, enriching, and helps us get along with our fellow human beings. Knowledge of science and technology, on the other hand, is highly useful as an economic and political tool. Knowledge of art, literature, and religion may also be useful as an economic and political tool, but such knowledge is not in the same league as that of science and technology. For this reason, our children need to learn both the uses and dangers of science and technology. That is, they need Forbidden Fruit served up in the cafeteria every day.

In my view, rational people, including schoolchildren,

should study the development of nuclear weapons and especially the bombing of Hiroshima and Nagasaki as examples of science and technology that cut both ways and continue to cut both ways. There is a world of easily accessible information available on everything from the Manhattan Project to the psychology and ecology of nuclear holocaust to the disposal of waste from nuclear power plants. Jonathon Schell's *Fate of the Earth* is a piece of nuclear doomsday literature that some have criticized as being shortsighted and alarmist now that the cold war has ended and the USSR no longer exists. The truth is that Schell's book is infinitely more well founded than that other popular doomsday book, namely Hal Lindsey's *Late Great Planet Earth*. Schell views the nuclear age as a time when knowledge allowed humanity to bring the energy machines of the stars home to planet Earth. We must now keep the stars (nuclear weapons) bottled up. His most telling point is that the *knowledge* of how to build such stars will never be lost. It is with us always. We can dismantle all our nuclear weapons, but we'll still, as a species, have eaten enough of the Tree of Knowledge to build more. Which, of course, is exactly what some non-superpower countries are trying to do as you read this page.

A simplistic view of nuclear technology is that American ingenuity and penchant for problem solving allowed us to develop and use these weapons before our enemies did, thus we won the war and kept the world safe for democracy. A more realistic view, and one theoretically available to the public schools, is that we did indeed develop nuclear weapons in response to a wartime situation, that we used them, that the costs and benefits of using them are still being debated, that their use issued in the cold war—with all its ramifications making their marks on John Kennedy's campaign speeches and Ronald Reagan's defense spending—that nuclear electrical power is a fringe benefit of weapons technology, and that, having brought the stars home to Earth we now must house them, dismantle them if we can, control their acquisition by petty despots hell-bent on vengeance, and dispose of the long-lived hazardous waste they generate as by-products. Knowledge—deep, broad, objective, sophisticated, cosmopolitan knowledge—not ignorance, is what we need to accomplish this task. These are the reasons nuclear technology is such wonderful instructional material.

ALTERNATIVES AND PROBLEMS

Parochial schools and home schools will never accomplish the job of education for society. They may work for some children, and these kids may turn out to be president. But with an ignorant public, he or she will face an impossible challenge. America needs an educated public, not a naive and mystic one. The human race needs an educated American public, if for no other reason than that we control—currently—so many of the world's weapons and resources. American public education is one of our nation's strongest and most useful assets, not one of our major liabilities.

But the value of an asset has its ups and downs, especially when managed incorrectly. American public schools have had some management problems of late, many of which arise from social forces outside the schools' control (e.g., drugs, easy access to hand weapons, economic decay, breakdown of family life, etc.). Those are only the management problems that get publicized. Equally severe, indeed if not far worse, management problems that the public schools cannot control are parental ignorance and parental religious fervor. These problems afflict even the most affluent and serene of public schools. Rational people asking why children seem so, well, *uneducated*, should visit a public school, visit its library, and ask the teachers about the ideas the students are being exposed to. If these ideas do not include the major controversial ones from all history, this school is in trouble.

Parental ignorance and religious fervor influence the manner in which teachers deal with subjects that elicit strong negative reactions. The net result is that subjects tend to be presented in rather bland ways that reinforce beliefs and values rather than challenge them. A teacher can't be exciting without challenging students' values. For example, we could present WWII as straight history, describing battles and their outcomes, with ultimate Allied victory over Germany, Italy, and Japan. Or, we could present WWII as an expected result of the shortsighted political events that followed WWI. And in the most exciting treatment of all, we could merge Paul Fussell's analysis of WWII *(Wartime)* into the history lessons, an act that would reveal war in all its violent stupidity, possibly even to the extent that a future president might remember the lessons. Each of these presentations has some validity, but the straight history without the human failure, or the human heroism, is damn boring.

Parental ignorance, however, probably overrides religious fervor as a problem for the public schools. When ignorance is coupled with economic deprivation, then the combination is deadly. By "ignorance" I mean lack of knowledge about how to be a good parent. I don't believe for a minute that good parenting and economic stability will turn today's youth into a corps of model children. Children, on the average, have never been "model" but have usually grown out of their difficult stages. The goal, it seems, should be to help them get through those difficult stages safely. I don't have a solution to this situation. I do have some recommendations about what to tell our children (see chapter 14), but those recommendations assume that we're already talking to them, treating them with a certain amount of respect, interacting with them in places other than the athletic field, and generally participating in their lives in an evident but nonintrusive manner.

Finally, some comments on prayer and Bible reading in the public classroom. Neither prayer nor the Bible will solve the problems of public education. Nor will a minute of silence, either, but nobody is harmed by a minute of silence. Prayer and the Bible are powerful devices subject to much abuse, especially in the structured and authoritarian setting of a classroom, primarily because the prayers are going to be Christian and the subjects of authority are going to be children. If there was any evidence that prayer and the Bible were effective tools for over-riding parental ignorance and religious fervor, then I'd suggest we get those tools back in the hands of teachers immediately.

But prayer in the public schools rings of self-delusionary logic. Just because something works for you personally, that doesn't mean it works for society. Prayer and the Bible are structured and authoritarian substitutes for an investigative and self-directed mind and as such have no place in the public schools. What the public schools need more than prayer is broadly educated and idealistic teachers, excitement, intellec-tual (not political) controversy, a reduction in the amount of em-phasis placed on athletics, and parents who *want* their children to read banned books so they can talk about why books get banned. In those kinds of schools, anyone can pray without fear.

ELEVEN

CRIME AND VIOLENCE

Even a rational person might legitimately ask, Why does the
United States of America, a nation blessed with abundance
in every way, seem plagued with an accelerating wave of violence that appears headed for a peak around the turn of the
Millennium? Are we seeing a preview of the end of the world?
The wash of blood across our newspaper pages and television
screens goes on forever. Why, oh why, are we murdering ourselves? These are some of the most powerful, honest, and important questions of our times, and almost everyone seems to
have an answer ranging from handgun control to putting the
Bible back into the classroom to the building of more prisons
to the lifetime incarceration of third-time felons. None of these
answers is necessarily correct.

PUNISHMENT AND DEVELOPMENT

It is not at all clear how to solve our problems of crime and violence. But it is very clear that American approaches to these
problems may well be founded in the philosophical underpin-
nings of Western Christianity, with its linear casuality, repen-

tance, punishment, forgiveness, and final judgment. Our child-rearing techniques and criminal codes both are built on the idea that if someone does something wrong, then he or she should be punished. The underlying assumption is that punishment results in altered behavior, namely the changing of wrong behavior to right behavior, permanently. But there is no inherent reason why a system that seems to work for child rearing should be expected to work when applied to criminals beyond the age of puberty, and in the case of crime and violence, there is plenty of evidence that this assumption is invalid.

All organisms, including humans, develop according to an inborn, individual as well as species-specific, genetic program that is itself the product of eons of evolutionary history. During the "reading and execution" of this program, the environment influences the form of the final product. This principle explains not only why childhood environment influences adult behavior, but also why, after an organism has reached adulthood, it may be exceedingly difficult, and often virtually impossible, to change traits that were established during childhood. There is no way to accurately predict which combination of genes and environmental factors will in fact produce a criminal. What we do know is that some environments tend to produce a higher level of criminal and violent behavior than do others. We also know that incarceration of a criminal at a distant time and site does not alter the environments that seem to produce the highest levels of criminal activity.

Western logic says: If Person X does wrong, then Person X should be punished. A post-Enlightenment corollary to this Western logic says that punishment *corrects* Person X's inclination to do wrong. Another corollary says that the threat of potential punishment *deters* an individual from doing something wrong. Thus our prisons are called "correctional facilities," often operated by departments of correction. Analogously, capital punishment is claimed to be a "deterrent" to capital crime. Because *we* (individual law abiders) are terrified of prison and the death penalty, we conclude *they* (the population of crooks) should be so terrified of prison and the electric chair that *they* refrain from criminal behavior. This logic breaks down because we law abiders tend to forget that a crook's best buddies and most sympathetic listeners are already in prison. The logic also breaks down, of course, because a criminal does not think in the same way as a law-abiding citizen; if he did, he wouldn't be a crook.

Religious conversion does occasionally function to radically alter unsocial behavior for the better. The only problem with religious conversion as a tool for criminal rehab is that the crook is usually already locked up, often for murder, when it happens. If the churches can actively convert social misfits into law abiding productive citizens before they become criminals, then the churches should have our support in this endeavor. They should have our support, that is, unless their definition of a productive citizen is one who believes Jesus is returning at midnight, December 31, 1999, so there's no need to live in an ecologically sound and reproductively responsible way, and that the Devil will be bound for a thousand years, and that all the sinners will be destroyed, and that God created the Earth in seven days in the year 4004 B.C. In other words, in the long run, irrational religious fundamentalism is a cure that's potentially as bad as a disease.

In his book *On Human Nature*, E. O. Wilson summarizes eloquently the enormous volume of knowledge at our disposal on the subject of human development. I won't digress into this massive body of literature from medicine and education in order to validate my prior point. I'm on solid ground when I claim that techniques for influencing the behavior of a prepubescent child are not necessarily those that will be effective in influencing that of a postpubescent criminal. I am not saying we should do away with prisons. I am saying that we should quit looking to prisons as a long-term solution to the problem of criminal violence in America. Prisons satisfy Western logic (punishment for wrongdoing) and exact formal, sanctioned vengeance. They do not now solve, nor have they ever in recorded history solved, the problem of crime and violence.

SOCIOLOGY AND PSYCHOLOGY OF VIOLENCE

The aforegoing discussion on prisons, correction, and violence is based mainly on published statistical analysis. The statistics on crime and violence do not cast a favorable light on the "correctional" system as a means of reducing violence at the population level (e.g., see *Time*, February 7, 1994, for a quick review). The probability of getting caught, convicted, receiving maximum sentence, actually fulfilling that sentence, and coming out of prison a changed and better person—socially fit instead of a social misfit—is shockingly low. Statistically speaking there is a surprisingly good chance a criminal will not get caught, not get convicted of the most serious charges that could be leveled against him, not serve his complete sentence in prison, and certainly not be trained or otherwise rehabilitated into a productive, employable, law-abiding citizen. Instead, there is an excellent chance that after a short time behind bars he will come out of prison a better crook, with just as much impetus to be a crook than before he went in.

The psychology of punishment for sin seems to work perfectly well for vast numbers of Christians, especially when the sins are the fact of having been born a human being, lusting after a neighbor's ass, and believing in evolution, and the punishment is (threatened) loss of eternal life. Statistically speaking, however, that same psychology does not work for society as a whole, especially on secular matters with more immediate consequences. It would be cynical of me to speculate that this psychology does not work on violent criminals because their goals fall far short of eternal life in heaven. But it's not all that cynical to claim that criminals' goals are often more tangible and immediate than heaven: money, drugs, power, the satisfaction of some unknown inner driving force.

There is little reason to believe, given the nature of the prison system in the United States, that convicted criminals' goals will change significantly as a result of their incarceration. All serious studies have arrived at this conclusion, including those conducted by the President's Commission on Law Enforcement and the Administration of Justice (1967), the National Advisory Commission on Civil Disorders (1967), the National Commission on the Causes and Prevention of Violence (1968), and a long list of subsequent scholars (e.g., those referenced by the Lynn Curtis and Elliott Currie books in the appendix), ranging from sociologists to mathematicians specializing in terrorism and national security. Televised interviews with recently released prisoners themselves—those shown on a recent *60 Minutes* episode, for example—mirror the scholars' findings. We don't rehabilitate very many, and the United States of America remains a "clear leader among modern stable democratic nations in its rates of homicide, assault, rape, and robbery." (Quote from report of the National Commission on the Causes and Prevention of Violence.)

It is not clear how much of our recent wave of violence is perpetrated as a result of planned criminal activity and how much occurs as a result of misdirected passions. A great deal of domestic violence is probably unplanned and evidently arises simply because people cannot get along with those that live in the same house or apartment. Failure to get along is of course a euphemism for some kind of deep anger that surfaces as spouse and child abuse, drinking, use of narcotics, and arguments that escalate into beatings and killings—the plotline for newspaper stories you read almost every day. In a significant number of cases, domestic violence ends up being directed at the police officer who responds to a call for help. When the shooting stops, people, including officers who responded to the call, are headed for the hospital or morgue.

Nor is it clear from a study of the literature that our present level of violence is actually significantly higher than in the past. For example, the statistical information to assess whether Jeffrey Dahmer was a product of the 1980s or whether his kind have always been with us is just not readily available. According to the accounts of anthropologists and missionaries, aboriginal cultures have practiced various kinds of violent behavior toward one another, including cannibalism, human sacrifice, and torture for centuries. The Aztecs were among the most violent people in history, regularly engaging in brutal human sacrifice for a multitude of reasons. In this century, totalitarian states have tortured, murdered, maimed, and otherwise abused literally millions of their own citizens (Idi Amin's Uganda; Joseph Stalin's Soviet Union). So the historical record suggests that violence and mayhem are as human as sex and religion, and it's mainly the form and circumstances of violence that seem to shift over time. The comparative question at the beginning of this chapter, however, still is of sobering and vital importance to our chances of surviving into the next millennium: Why is the United States a more violent and imprisoned nation than those that are seemingly our peers? If you have the answer to that question—the real answer—please tell the individual who is president at the time you read this book.

WEAPONS

The United States is not only a violent place but also a heavily armed one. Our Second Amendment has grown into a monster, spawning legions of weapons-toting hunters and a powerful weapons lobby. There is a move afoot, in the 1990s, to remove some of these weapons from general circulation and to make it more difficult for a person to obtain a gun. Assault rifles and handguns are the main targets of these efforts, which range from the so-called Brady Bill (mandating background checks and waiting periods for those wishing to buy handguns), to gun buybacks and trade-ins (for cash, gift certificates, meals). The Brady Bill and buybacks are noble endeavors. If they save a single human life, they will be worth the effort and expense. But they are bear-at-the-cave-door acts that are not going to reduce the weapons supply very substantially, because individual weapons have a very long life expectancy. In fact, the most important effect of gun control efforts may be a cultural one. By focusing attention on the weapons problem, these activities alter public perception of the seriousness of that problem. And, it is serious.

The statistics tell us that buying a handgun for protection increases the chance of being killed with that same gun, often by someone we know. The handgun purchase also increases the probability that one of our children or their playmates will be killed accidently with that same weapon. Again, the American logic applied to crime and violence (buy a handgun for protection) often fails when put into practice (shot by a paramour with one's own gun). Americans will continue to fight over gun control, simply because of our culturally based approach to problem solving, namely, see a problem, remove the problem. See a gun used to kill someone, remove the gun. See a gun used to solve a problem, use guns to solve problems. See an international political problem, send in the army. Studies show that there is a relationship between gun possession and potential for loss of life during a criminal act. But studies also show that there is a distinct, powerful, and hard relationship between the existence of drug addiction and a socioeconomic underclass in a seemingly affluent society and a whole spectrum of other social problems, including crime and violence.

Handguns are also notoriously dangerous to their owners who are old, lonely, depressed, and sick, regardless of how criminal their minds may be. Automobiles are equally dangerous to their owners, of all ages, but more often to young, male ones than to females in their fifties. Like all dangers—disease, accidental death, exposure to toxic and/or radioactive chemicals—violence is not evenly distributed among the population but everyone in the population has the potential for becoming a victim. The bottom line is that the United States of America has evolved into a gun-toting, drug-taking, energy-gulping society that has a great many wonderful attributes and opportunities and lives in a beautiful and bountiful land. We have also evolved into a complicated, often paradoxical, society, characterized by enormous inertia. The evolutionary principles state very clearly that one does not make fundamental changes in such entities very quickly. If you've evolved into an elephant, taking away your gun and putting you in jail for a year will not make you a gazelle.

A (NOT SO NEW) ONTOGENETIC SUGGESTION

The only real way to reduce levels of violence and crime is to alter the childhood environments that produce criminals. When we bash society's efforts to provide safe neighborhoods, exciting education, and decent employment possibilities as "one more liberal giveaway" while demanding that elected officials "get tough on crime, build more prisons, and lock up the three-time felons for life," then we're part of the problem instead of the solution. There is a substantial amount of evidence that secure, drug-free neighborhoods, decent and exciting education, a certain level of economic stability, and obvious opportunities for long-term meaningful employment all function to significantly reduce (not necessarily eliminate) violent crime. The take-home lesson is this: If we want to perpetuate a criminal class in America, we should build more prisons and do nothing else; if we want to reduce the levels of violence and crime in our nation, we have to stop raising children under conditions that turn them into criminals and violent people.

TWELVE

HUMANISM

H*umanism* is a word that is anathema to the religious right, although its loathsome qualities can be multiplied many times over simply by adding the redundant word *secular* in front of it. The debate over secular humanism, especially as it is supposedly taught in the public schools, is worthy of some attention. Secular humanism is a body of thought that attributes a certain measure of free will to human beings, and in turn holds us accountable for our actions. But members of the radical religious right typically do not believe humans should be so arrogant as to claim to have free will and independent minds, and therefore derive morality and accountability from God, i.e., the Bible, which, of course, is also filled with human thoughts and ideas.

Humanism is thus a body of thought that is defined, if not created, by religion, so that we cannot talk about humanism except in terms of religion's relationship to it. Furthermore, the debate is fueled not by humanists, who tend to counterattack rather than attack, or by scholarly theologians, who tend to accept that religion is a peculiarly human phenomenon and study it as such, but by those with a religious political agenda. Like most religion-based political agendas, this one seeks to put in place mechanisms for directing the behavior of the masses. Such mechanisms generally fail after generating enormous amounts of misery regardless of whether they are religion-based or not.

Most of the books that explain and defend humanism are well written, thoughtful, sometimes almost academic texts (e.g., Paul Kurtz's *In Defense of Secular Humanism*). Most of the books that attack humanism are shallow and strident, as are many typical letters to the editor in local newspapers. The discussion most commonly focuses on the public schools. One rarely hears much of an outcry against secular humanism except in the context of curricula, library materials, and teacher behavior. Sex education is a favorite target. School library materials that have been attacked include some American classics such as J. D. Salinger's *Catcher in the Rye*. Condemned teacher behavior includes attendance at conferences on the political influence of the religious right in the public schools. I'm guessing that teachers who attended a conference on the subject of how to counter undue influence exerted by athletic boosters might also catch some flak, but such criticism would quickly fade from public and institutional memory.

FREE WILL

The question of whether humans have free will has been discussed and debated for centuries, and by some of the finest minds to be found among the ranks of philosophers. However, the question has also been answered for an equally long time: We do. Humans are free to act as they please. They've been doing it for as long as there have been humans, and their ancestors probably did it, too. On the other hand, actions stemming from the exercise of free will have historically been limited by nature, and with the advent of social groups, by tradition, customs, and laws. We have the free will to strip off our clothes in Anchorage, Alaska, and jump in the ocean with the intent of swimming to Rio. In this case, nature ultimately will make us responsible for our act. So, too, do we have the free will to commit murder, and like nature, the legal system (one hopes) will try very hard to make us ultimately accountable for our act.

So we have free will, but one of the hallmarks of civilization is that we do not have complete freedom to exercise it without consequence. On the other hand, being human, we also have (at least in theory) the power to anticipate these consequences, evaluate them, and use them to establish a code of behavior toward our fellow humans. That is, we have the power, regardless of whether we have the inclination, to use our knowledge and experience to construct a set of socially acceptable morals and ethics. The religious right, however, holds that all consequences stem from violating the dictates of the Scriptures and that the schools should be teaching biblical values and morals. In essence, they're saying that theory breaks down in practice, that humans *will* not exercise their powers and thus do not really have such powers.

The empirical evidence suggests the fundamentalists may be right in part; that is, immoral behavior has been a feature of human existence for all recorded history. And, in fairness to the fundamentalists, even humanists must admit that in the United States, Western Christianity provides the most easily accessible, reliable, and commonly accepted moral codes available to the average citizen. Indeed, all religions assume an ideal of goodness instead of evil. Yet there is an equal body of evidence that neither religion nor humanism has been able to control the masses completely or forever. Furthermore, humanists are quick to detect the use of religion as a weapon, especially a political one. Humans have never been reluctant to use their weapons, be they verbal, ideological, or material. Thus the fight over humanism is not likely to end so long as people use strong religious beliefs to guide their political actions.

THE APES REVISITED

It is an interesting philosophical exercise to imagine a completely humanist life, that is, without religion. Scientists call this kind of exercise a thought experiment, and it is one of their more useful tools. Given the basic nature of the human species, that is, its genetically determined traits, would we develop civilized societies without religion? Of course we have historical examples of supposedly atheistic states, such as was the former Soviet Union, but those are not valid case studies because they were legalistic structures superimposed on societies that already had fairly strong religions. For our experiment, we need a case in which a human society evolves in the complete absence of religion. The closest examples of such societies are those of the various nonhuman primates.

Most monkey and ape societies have rather well established rules that dictate the roles individuals play in the group, allow for those roles to change, and allow us to predict the outcomes of certain behaviors. In truth, monkey and ape societies, which we can assume do not have religion, nevertheless *do* have limits to and consequences of behaviors. What they may not have is a deep appreciation for and understanding of these constraints in the human sense. That is, we're not certain how skillfully baboons evaluate the long-term consequences of their behavioral options. We are certain that if a baboon exceeds the limits of its behavioral options, it gets in trouble.

On the other hand, the particular behaviors exhibited by monkeys and apes may not fit within human moral codes, so that we might be inclined to deny the fact that the nonreligious monkeys have constraints on their behaviors. So in order to perform and analyze our thought experiment, we need to separate social constraints per se from any specific kind of constraints. Information about nonhuman primates can be found in abundance in any reasonably sized library. After a careful study of this information, I've come to the following conclusions:

1. Yes, nonhuman primates have all kinds of constraints and socially acceptable, as well as unacceptable, behaviors.
2. A monkey does not violate the behavioral constraints of its society without suffering consequences.
3. Species of monkeys and apes differ in both their "personalities" and in their social structures (i.e., in their behavioral constraints).
4. Individual monkeys and apes also differ in their personalities, too. Thus when we become acquainted with them, they are as individually distinct as our more human friends.

To be completely honest, the nonreligious monkeys and apes sound a lot like us, with our various societies and cultures, when described in these general terms. Yes, I must conclude, without religion we would evolve "moral" codes that would establish behavioral constraints. My educated guess is that such codes would be more a product of our respective environment and gender differences in physical stature than of our minds. I'm also guessing we'd end up calling these codes "religion."

MORALITY AND ECONOMY

Would human nonreligious moral codes be anything at all like the ones we now supposedly have? Nobody knows. But if the anthropological literature tells us anything of value relative to religion, it's that religious systems are an integral part of the overall adaptation that various societies have with their environments, and particularly with those aspects of their environments that dictate the food economy.

Did agriculture contribute significantly to the development of the world's great religions by freeing humans from the restrictions their local environments placed on their food economy? Maybe. Such an agricultural effect, if present, may be so deeply buried in our past as to be unrecoverable. There is well-known evidence that the (apparently) nonagricultural Neanderthals had practices we would interpret as religious, at least with respect to the burial of their dead, so that religion per se is much more deeply embedded in the human genome than knowledge of how to grow corn. Nevertheless, agriculture separates large numbers of people from the chimpanzee-level interactions with their environments. By freeing spirituality from local environments, agriculture allows the export and storage of both food and ideas. Agriculture also allows the growth of populations. That is, when a society can grow and store food, it can start to grow more humans, which viewed scientifically are, in fact, stored food (potential energy). The discussion always seems to get back (down) to sex, doesn't it?

SEX AND THE TEN COMMANDMENTS

Humanism inspires its most fervent discussion when the subject is sex. It is especially galling to the religious right, and indeed to many moderates, that as a result of the church-state separation clause of our constitution, as well as various court rulings, we can teach sex education but not the Ten Commandments in the public schools. (In my clipping file, this last phrase is perhaps the most common one found in letters to the editor, as in "we can teach sex but not the Ten Commandments.") On the other hand, we have many laws and moral codes that are based on the Ten Commandments, so that the Commandments are not altogether missing from secular affairs. We have laws against murder and theft. Adultery results in divorce, reconciliation, or more adultery, and often civil litigation (consequences). We have laws against bearing false witness (perjury, fraud). Any of these subjects, supplemented by material from a local daily newspaper, would make a wonder-

ful series of lessons in a social studies class. What we're not allowed to teach are the first five Commandments (first five
Protestant = first four Catholic), and the last commandment
(last Protestant = last two Catholic) about covetousness. However, greed is an excellent subject for secular education, lends
itself well to fiction, and is often addressed in literature classes.

The first four Protestant Commandments address the con-
solidation of God's power over humans (as if a God that made
the known universe needed to consolidate His/Her/Its power).
The fifth (Protestant) Commandment is somewhat enigmatic:
"Honor your father and your mother, that your days may be
prolonged in the land which the Lord your God gives you."
(New American Standard Bible, Exodus 20:12.) The best way
to teach the fifth Commandment is to gather some statistics on
single-parent families (see *Time* magazine cover story, June 20,
1994). Aside from the warning about adultery, and coveting
your neighbor's wife, the Ten Commandments say nothing
about sex, especially teenage unmarried, unwanted-pregnancy-
generating sex.

I contend that the sex education vs. Ten Commandments
case is but a specific instance of the more general question of
whether the possession of knowledge encourages humans to use
it. In other words, if I take a course in auto mechanics, am I encouraged to work on my car? This question is an important one
because of the many analogous questions that can be asked at
all levels. For example, if we build weapons, are we encouraged
to use them? Or, if we learn how babies are made, are we inclined to make some? If we learn how to avoid making babies,
are we encouraged to engage in sex? If the answer to both of
these last two questions is "yes," then maybe we should look for
something other than sex education to blame for young unmarried, unwanted-pregnancy-generating sex.

It is proper to ask, too, whether this last question above has
the same underlying structure as the others. The answer, of
course, is no. The evidence is fairly clear that school-age children are increasingly engaging in sex with or without the knowl-

edge of how to avoid making babies, or at least without apply-
ing that knowledge if they possess it. If you work on your car
without the proper knowledge, you're very likely to simply
screw it up and have to take it (sheepishly) to a real mechanic.
In other words, when you're tinkering with machinery, ignorance virtually guarantees failure. In the case of sex, however,
ignorance virtually guarantees success (at making babies).

Given this observation, the debate over secular humanism
seems to become one of control rather than morals per se. That
is, sex, not babies, is the focus of the religious right. The social
problem is children having children; the moral problem, according to some, is children having sex. Statistically the two
problems—social and moral—are correlated, but the former is
also strongly correlated with levels of ignorance about birth
control, or at least with levels of disinclination to use birth control methods. A friend sent an interesting clipping a few months
ago that illustrated what I'm talking about. His state legislature's
female members formed a group to study the ways teenage
pregnancy might be reduced. One of the members heartily en-
dorsed the move, "so long as the recommendations did not include the use of contraceptives." A secular humanist would
translate that condition as follows: "In my role as a member of
the governing body, I'll help solve a major social problem so
long as the solution doesn't violate my personal religious beliefs." In that statement lies a strong merger of church and state,
a *de facto* violation of the First Amendment ban on such link-
ages.

HUMANISM VERSUS RELIGION

Humanism has been labeled both a religion and a work of the
Devil by religious ultraconservatives. At issue is the question of
who has power over the universe—God or humans. "The universe" in this case becomes more inclusive the more one believes
the answer is God. And in extreme cases, those who seek to

make the term *universe* all-inclusive cannot be distinguished from those who seek absolute power—human power—over the lives of others. It is a long distance from the Big Bang to the bedroom, but if we believe those who interpret the word of God for us, the Creator who generated the Milky Way and a billion other galaxies is the same God who condemns the use of contraceptives by women in the developing world. Surely, if indeed humanity is the work of a Supreme Being, there is a point in human affairs in which our God-given gifts of intelligence, insight, memory, emotion, creativity, and understanding can serve as guides to responsible behavior, both at the individual and the population level. And at that point, we become humanists.

THIRTEEN

UTOPIAS

For a scholar interested in intellectual history, a study of utopias would provide a lifetime of captivating, fascinating, mind-boggling, and at times utterly depressing exploration. Few ideas illustrate the extremes of human idealism and frailty as well as that of the utopia—the imaginary perfect place where everyone is happy, healthy, beautiful, well fed, and safe; where all laws are just and all behavior is moral; and where there are no toxic chemicals, radioactive wastes, or one-point losses in championship basketball games. It is an uplifting experience just to think about the wonderful heights to which the human spirit can soar when building a utopia, a measure of what we could be if only we *would* manifest our finest traits.

But it's also a downer to realize how easily humans are duped into buying someone else's version of utopia. Suddenly we appear almost primeval, deprived of our humanity, when kneeling before a charismatic leader who promises everything. Hitler's Germany was the cruelest of modern utopian jokes. Marx claimed heaven to be the most narcotic of utopias. Throughout history, politicians have ridden our credulity to power, then proved time and again that utopias exist only in the human mind. If rational people do nothing else in life, they will at least be highly suspicious of other people, including politicians and televangelists who promise religious relief from all the major and minor irritations associated with having been born a human being on planet Earth.

UTOPIA DEFINED

Taken most strictly, the word *utopia* refers to an entire kingdom. But the danger lies not in buying the heaven-on-earth idea, which most people understand is simply a dream, but in buying into smaller schemes that have utopian properties. In modern society, there are two areas—namely religion and politics—in which utopian elements are pervasive, subtle, addictive, diversionary, and dangerous. And when we mix religion and politics, we've got a real mess. On the other hand, there are utopian qualities every citizen can help bring about in a society. These qualities sound remarkably like the American Dream as revealed in the United States Constitution, i.e., almost mainline moderate Protestant, but when applied uniformly, sound rather liberal and outright humanist.

UTOPIA FILLED TO THE BRIM

Very little in our religious traditions deals directly with the overriding problems of our times—overpopulation, environmental deterioration, violent crime, drugs, war, and ignorance. Many people will bristle when I make that assertion, some because they feel that if everybody would just accept Jesus as their personal savior, all these problems would go away, others because I've included overpopulation in my list of overriding problems. If you accept Jesus as your personal savior, the problems of drugs, overpopulation, environmental deterioration, violent crime, war, and ignorance might indeed go away *for you*. They will not go away for the rest of humanity, however, and ultimately that one big problem—overpopulation—will eventually get bad enough regardless of whether everyone on Earth accepts Jesus as their personal savior or not, so that the world will begin to look a great deal like that predicted by John of Patmos, the author of Revelation. That doesn't mean the biblical predictions are necessarily true or foreordained; it simply means that when humans run out of food and shelter they die miserably, just like other animals do.

UTOPIAN BABIES

A chapter on utopias seems like a strange place to digress into the subject of birth control, especially on the individual level, but babies have a way of becoming heavily involved in our large and small utopian dreams. The religious right, and indeed most mainline Christians, view sexual abstinence prior to marriage as highly desirable behavior, and indeed the solution to many of our social problems. In this case, the religious right is correct. Young people are well advised, for any number of valid reasons having nothing to do with sin, to delay their sexual activity until they are mature enough to cope with the consequences. Young sex is not utopia. It is, however, biology at work, which should in itself serve as a warning to those preoccupied with young sex for whatever reason.

In practice, unwanted pregnancy and unwanted disease can both be avoided, socially and individually, through abstinence. However, it's not at all clear *how* to teach young people to behave in abstemious ways. What is clear is that the events leading to sexual deviation from the straight and narrow path of abstinence are complicated, sometimes inexplicable, multifaceted, and not always easily controlled. It is also clear that some of the most effective methods for reducing unwanted pregnancy as a social problem are anathema to the conservative right. I digress into the subject of birth control not because it's my personal soapbox (although overpopulation comes close), but because it is actually an excellent model system for the study of mechanisms causing the collapse of utopias.

In fact, being a virgin at marriage guarantees virtually nothing else about that marriage. Being a virgin at marriage does not guarantee happiness, a high level of long-term compatibility, financial success, a clean kitchen and three balanced meals a day, fun, romance, healthy children, or anything else. It only guarantees that the woman is not and has never been pregnant and reduces the chances that partners are carrying venereal infections. In placing such a high value on one largely symbolic property (virginity) of a system (marriage), we ignore the rather obvious fact that the symbolic property has little real connection to the day-to-day, year-after-year events that control the long-term survival of the system itself. The virginity/marriage model can be generalized to provide an explanation for why utopias fail. They are delusional dreams that divert our minds away from the real factors that control the quality of our lives.

A SIMPLE UTOPIAN PRINCIPLE

The real factors that control the quality of human lives are the energy supply, the water supply, and what I'll summarize under the abstract name of intellectual domain. The energy supply includes food, shelter, and transportation, because all of these basic needs are in turn dependent on energy. In the United States, food is mainly Middle East petroleum converted into wheat, corn, soybeans, cattle, and chickens. Shelter is mainly cellulose (= lumber = potential energy), steel and aluminum (produced, transported, and processed at great energy expense), and brick (produced and transported at great energy expense). Transportation obviously involves the consumption of petroleum, coal, and electricity. Here's a simple mathematical utopian principle: The more wheat, corn, beef, chicken, petroleum, steel, aluminum, and transportation you possess, the higher your standard of living, the freer you are from infectious disease, and the closer you are to utopia.

We fight wars over energy, the most blatantly illustrative of them being the Persian Gulf War with Iraq. But most well-educated people know that oil is not the most important liquid resource of the next millennium. Water is the resource whose supply will dictate the standards of living of massive numbers of humans, including those in the United States. Fresh water differs from oil in that water cannot be easily transported tens of thousands of miles to fuel the war machines and agricultural technology of a utopian nation. Why not? Because the energy needed to transport petroleum comes from the petroleum supply itself. The energy needed to transport water, however, also comes from petroleum. But even more significant than the energy costs of water transport are the technological and ecological problems associated with water transport. And people who have water always fight to keep it. Finally, water-borne diseases are very common, spread easily, and tend to attack the youngest humans. So for a variety of reasons, utopian dreams are highly vulnerable to their water supplies.

We now come to the matter of intellectual domains. *Intellectual* refers to the mind; a *domain* is a "territory over which dominion is exercised," or "a sphere of influence or activity," according to my dictionary. *Territory* and *sphere* in this case are metaphors, referring to a bounded space or set of conditions. An intellectual domain is an environment in which a mind lives according to certain rules and regulations.

Rich intellectual domains let our minds live in freedom, exploring all the nooks and crannies, hidden places, grand vistas, the good and bad, beautiful and ugly. Impoverished intellectual domains restrict our minds to certain avenues, keeping us out of fenced-in places that are defined as dangerous and dictate not only our questions, but also our answers. We've come to the basic utopian paradox: *Real* utopias are rich intellectual domains, yet the qualities that make these domains rich are often anathema to most people who claim to be leading us into utopia. I don't need to talk around the subject. Ultraconservative, politically successful fundamentalist religions claim to offer utopia but actually restrict our minds to certain avenues, keep us out of fenced-in places deemed dangerous, and choose not only our questions, but also our answers. Prisons accomplish the same thing, as do totalitarian political regimes.

THE UNITED STATES OF UTOPIA

In the United States of America, the most welcome utopian dream would be for every child to be wanted, supported adequately, taken to a competent physician when ill, encouraged in his or her personal intellectual development, exposed in a supportive and educational way to the frailties of human existence, taught self-esteem, taught how to make his or her accommodations with sex, and provided with interesting books, a safe walk to school, concerned teachers, and loving, patient but stern-when-need-be parents. Instead, so often, they get athletics, guns, drugs, inanity, and in a depressing number of cases, poverty and inadequate medical care to boot. The solutions to poverty, and all the misery it entails, are not easy to come by, yet a nation's utopian dreams crumble when a significant fraction of its citizens do not have access to those dreams. We don't know what that fraction is. It could be far smaller than many of us want to believe. Five-tenths of one percent of the American population is in prison, and we admit to having a socially disruptive crime wave. Five-tenths of one percent of anything is not a large fraction.

If there is a place on Earth called utopia, it is a fragile, ephemeral, and highly localized place generated partly by luck and maintained by an individual or a small group of people often related by birth or marriage. In other words, the more power over our own lives that we've acquired by hard work and the circumstances of birth, the more ability we have to construct our own personal version of utopia here on Earth. But earthly utopias are ephemeral—that is one of the most persistent lessons of history. Enjoy them while you can. Give some private and sober thought to the social and political responsibilities of a well-educated and fortunate citizen. And read history. Our own personal utopias are most secure when certain of their properties—security, meaningful employment, challenging literature, freedom to speak, read, and assemble—are spread throughout the society in which we live.

UTOPIA OF THE MIND

If there is an ultimate utopia—heaven—it is to be found for certain in the same place as God, namely in the minds of believers, and its existence beyond the minds of believers is as likely, or unlikely, as the existence of the God of the Big Bang. But as is the case with all utopias, the heaven of the mind can be converted into the heaven of the political process quite easily. A sure clue this transition has taken place is the use of religion-based moral arguments in fights over such earthly items as school library materials, art, and private sexual behavior between consenting adults.

Lawrence LeShan's book *The Psychology of War* (see appendix) addresses the subject of utopias in an elegant and eloquent manner. His analysis provides a clear warning of the dangers that lie lurking in the perfect mythical worlds we create in our collective mind. Although his subject is war, he repeatedly refers to the utopian images used by various political leaders to incite nations into brutal conflicts. From the "war to end all wars" (WWI) to the "New World Order" (George Bush's description of the anticipated results of the Persian Gulf War), wars have been fought by nations pitting themselves (ultimate good) against others (ultimate evil), for a grand and glorious permanently changed world to follow the victory that both sides consider the only possible outcome. It never happens. It didn't happen after World War I, it didn't happen after World War II, it didn't happen after the Persian Gulf War, and it won't happen after the next war, either, whatever that one is about.

In a prior book, *Einstein's Space and Van Gogh's Sky*, LeShan makes a strong case for multiple reality domains (e.g., the domain of history, the domain of art, the domain of physics). The rules for establishing reality and communicating ideas are different in each of these domains. What passes for a fact in art is not necessarily a fact in science. In *The Psychology of War*, LeShan tells us that wars are fought so frequently because societies slip easily from sensory reality into mythical reality. Individual humans regularly operate in several domains of reality during a day's work, always living with a conflict between the need to be independent and the need to belong to a larger, grander scheme of things. Independent life corresponds to one in the sensory universe; membership in a grand scheme corresponds to life in a mythical-equals-mental universe. The human is such a spiritual animal anyway, that the transition from sensory domain (pieces of hands and legs and your child's face strewn on a battlefield) to mythical one (Armageddon with us as the good guys) becomes dangerously easy. All we need is a leader to put us in the "right" mood; then the debate ceases over whether we should purposefully create hell knowing full well we're under the delusion that we're making heaven. At this point, anyone who calls the mythical utopia by its real name—*living hell*—is suddenly a traitor.

Our dreams and desires of grandeur are among our most noble, yet among our most threatening, of traits. Survival beyond midnight, December 31, 1999, might well demand that we view ourselves as if from afar, adopt the courage that accompanies distance, and declare that the millennium is only one more day in a long history of days in which we wake, make our living, and seek both a meaningful individual life and a non-pathological sense of purpose. The line between nobility and degeneracy is easily crossed by those seeking heaven on Earth. Paradox lies on either side of it; on the noble side of the line, the paradox is frustrating, while on the degenerate side it is downright dangerous.

As I have said many times throughout this book, it is not easy to have been born a human being. Most of us believe it is more interesting to have been born a human than a member of any other species, but that belief is fairly inconsequential because we cannot change the fact of our birth. We are humans, like it or not. Our right and privilege in this human condition is to believe whatever we want to believe; our obligation is to act in a publicly responsible way. The fact of our birth means we have no choice but to compromise, to reconcile beliefs with public responsibilities. Many of us think we've done that. If we can read a banned book without wanting to shut down the library or walk through an art gallery without condemning the taxes spent to support the place, then we've come pretty close. And if we live in a society in which the majority of people can do the same, then we're in utopia.

PART III
ADVICE AND
RECOMMENDATIONS

FOURTEEN

THINKING BIG/ACTING SMALL

What can we do about the seemingly monumental problems of our times? This is a question that needs to be asked as well as answered. The first thing we can do is ask it, raise it as a topic of conversation in our various social encounters, make it a point of discussion with our children, parents, teachers, friends, and anyone who is in a position of decision-making power. The second thing we can do is answer it. The answer is *something*. *Something* is a better answer than *nothing*. The *something* involves local and immediate actions at least, done on a small and personal scale, with the intent, indeed the idealism, of changing the world into a safer, saner place before the Millennium arrives.

BIG TALK

One thing anyone can do is convert small talk into big talk. There are times when small talk is highly appropriate, but there are some times when small talk is highly inappropriate, such as private sit-down dinners with well-educated friends. This distinction is one of the rules of etiquette usually not covered in books ostensibly dealing with that subject. Most etiquette books tell you how to make out wedding invitations and set the table; these are important subjects, to be sure, but they are nowhere as important as what to talk about with well-educated, professionally successful friends.

Most of my friends in the business community, in the legal and medical professions, and in positions of major administrative responsibility, have very little to say. Neither do their wives. As a group, the doctors are, in my view, among the most unconversant of all. They make excellent livings; some are exceedingly wealthy; virtually to a person they are among the most admired, respected, and well-educated people in our society. Yet they rarely if ever speak out on any subject unless it has a direct impact on their profession, especially the business aspects of it. What are they afraid of? Losing their patients? Occasionally we hear about one who's taken a public and idealistic stand on some issue of importance, some issue worthy of their expertise. Most often we hear massive silence from the rest.

I attend numerous social occasions with some of the more successful people of my community—physicians, attorneys, CEOs of local corporations, heads of local government agencies. At one of these events recently held in a truly magnificent new home, I saw the bartender listening intently to a small group of men, a group that included a leading heart specialist and two highly successful attorneys. Later I asked this bartender what these men were talking about. He answered: golf, Hillary Clinton, and dirty jokes. Then he added: but some of the dirty jokes were about Hillary Clinton. I'd guessed as much. That's the same conversation I'd heard at a previous gathering where some men in similar professional positions had been seated at a table together. Suppose Hillary Clinton, Joycelyn Elders, Janet Reno, and Anita Hill found themselves together at a social event. Would they spend two hours huddled in the kitchen talking about recipes and telling off-color Norman Schwartzkopf jokes? Maybe, but I doubt it.

When I suggest to my well-educated financially successful

friends that they budget ten percent of their conversational time for big talk, they usually laugh and go on talking about sports. Typically we're at dinner somewhere, their wives have labored all day to put out a competitive spread, and the wine bottles are down to fumes when my friends get told that all their past several hours' worth of conversation about football, golf, their children, yard, pets, etcetera, is not what they should be talking about. The men think I'm trying to be funny. The women get mad; they all have college degrees and most were in some honor society, but they don't want to be told that their competitive cooking and table setting are not big enough concerns for them in today's world. But ten percent is not much of a goal. That's only six minutes out of every hour's worth of conversation. One of America's most serious problems is right in our own living room—we spend our time on small, instead of big, subjects. This is a problem anyone can begin to solve now.

LETTERS

Anyone also can write some meaningful letters, especially to well-educated financially successful friends who are hiding behind their education and success. It's okay to enclose clippings, editorials, and political cartoons with your own commentary about them. My ultraconservative relatives send I-told-you-so type clippings that simply reinforce biases and narrow political beliefs. I tend to avoid Thomas Sowell and Cal Thomas columns in favor of those that present rational and intellectually honest visions. During the fall of 1993, for example, Dr. Joycelyn Elders, Surgeon General of the United States, suggested that we study (*study*) the legalization of certain drugs. In my experience, *study* of an issue almost always reveals alternative ways to solve problems, especially if such study helps eliminate self-delusion as a major factor clouding the issue. From the conservatives' reaction, however, you'd have thought she'd suggested castration of the pope. A few editorial writers, however, noted that Americans have a predilection for self-delusion, and that given the monumental burden that illegal narcotics place on our society, maybe some statistical analysis would help clarify the issues. These are the kinds of clippings to send to your well-educated friends.

SIMPLICITY AND COMPLEXITY

One truly effective way to redirect social conversations is to convert simplistic world views into their more complex counterparts. Most issues of global importance are not simple at all, but very complex. An outstanding example is the simplistic world view summarized by the words "stop abortion now." The abortion issue is a national hot button wired to an exceedingly convoluted set of social conditions. You may be opposed to abortion. Fine. It's your right to be so opposed and your privilege, if not duty, to try to influence the political activities of your nation accordingly. On the other hand, the issue itself is not a yes/no type phenomenon. The reasons why people get pregnant are highly varied, and the reasons they seek abortion are equally so. Yes, we can reduce the pregnancy to unprotected sex, or faulty contraceptives, as it sometimes happens. But we cannot generalize the reasons why people engage in unprotected sex, or for that matter, protected sex, kinky sex, fun sex, or no sex. Nor can we separate the issue of a woman's right to a clean, safe medical procedure that allows her to continue building a successful and productive life for herself from the issue of the rights of an unborn child. This factor alone guarantees that the abortion issue will never be resolved.

Nobody can solve the problems of unwanted pregnancy, politically hot abortion rights, or teenage motherhood during ten percent of the evening's conversation. What anyone can do is expose a small group of well-educated people, some of whom may be in positions of major responsibility over the lives of others, to a meaningful, objective, information-laden conversation that hopefully erodes their simplistic and highly personal views of the world down into a more realistic, complex, and sophisticated one. In other words, the task is to shape and enlarge our friends' views so that they match our friends' levels of education and success. The device for accomplishing this task need not be the abortion debate. Controversial art, evolution, school library materials, national energy policy are all perfectly useful, and effective, subjects.

IDEAS

Ideas are what the evolutionary biologists call memes, that is, mental constructs that seem to take on lives of their own, rather like germs that get passed from person to person. Anyone can become a source of intellectual infections that spread throughout his or her local population. Of course anyone can also become a source of bad and stupid ideas as well as good and mutually beneficial ones. But I'm not very worried about that happening; a reader who's gotten this far in this book is unlikely to become a source of stupid ideas. And, I'm convinced, the reading list in the appendix will crowd out the really bad ideas and replace them rather quickly with some relatively mature ones.

Here are some specific suggestions about ways to pick up interesting ideas. These suggestions may seem pretty trivial at first, but remember, we're acting small while thinking big.

1. Go to the natural history museum. Natural history museums are illuminating and wondrous buildings, sources of material for casual conversation, and great places to take children or visiting dignitaries.

My friends often express disdain for natural history museums, but I usually then get very affronted. For example, here is a conversation I had recently with the president of a successful local company. He has a college degree. He majored in business and wrote his first (two-page) paper as a college senior in the late 1950s.

FRIEND: Hey, what'd you do when you were in Denver?

JB: We went to the museum and the art gallery.

F: Jeez; I coulda got you tickets to a Nuggets game.

JB: My wife and I don't give a damn about a Nuggets game. We had a great time at the museum and the art gallery.

F: I heard that place has one o' them theaters where it's best if you got a couple o' beers under your belt before you go in. Y'know? Like on a rocket ship? Heh-heh-heh-heh.

JB: Actually, I spent most of my time in the insect displays. I think my wife was down in geology; she loves those rocks.

F: Yeah, them women love rocks! Got any diamonds? Heh-heh-heh.

No need to continue this conversation much further. The simple truth is that for very little money and equally small amounts of time, zoos and natural history museums offer anyone a rather expansive view of the world. After a half dozen visits to various natural history museums, a person begins to understand that great size and strength do not guarantee survival forever, that familiar patterns—recognizable starfish and clams—have been present on Earth for hundreds of millions of years, and that if an organism is to survive in a particular environment, then adaptation is a necessity.

> 2. Go to an art museum. Only in an art museum do we come to see how truly important, lasting, and unique are the products of single individuals. Art museums put governments, corporations, dicta-

tors and tyrants, kings and princes, arrogance and disdain all in their places. There on the wall is a painting—oil on canvas, watercolor on paper—that expresses an individual vision, a particular set of thoughts, ideas, metaphors. The museum has paid what seems like an enormous amount of money for . . . for what? For one individual human being's view of the world, be it the outer physical world, or the inner mental one, in which he or she may also have lived. An afternoon in the galleries will show you, unequivocally, how truly important your own personal contribution to this world can be. The art museum is the place where your personal worth, as an individual, is declared—boldly, strikingly, in a "vocabulary" that transcends the words of hot-button politics—by people whom you've never met, that may have lived centuries before your time, and may have come from cultures as foreign to yours as any from the realm of science fiction.

3. Read a nonfiction book. In fact, read several. Browse from the list in the appendix of this book, find one that sounds intriguing, and try it. My own recommendation is to read one serious nonfiction book for every piece of fiction read. In general, nonfiction that is well written and adequately documented will quickly turn anyone into a much more sophisticated person than he or she is now. Marc Reisner's *Cadillac Desert* and Neil Sheehan's *A Bright Shining Lie* are two excellent examples of "must-read" nonfiction. These books are a little heavy in places but are otherwise very well written and extensively documented. They also deal with two of the major events of the post–WWII era: the exploitation of our natural resources and Vietnam (not necessarily connected).

4. Subscribe to, and read, a serious magazine, for example the *New Yorker* or *Art in America*. These also are available in most public libraries, free. Library cards are generally free, too. Even for children. At most libraries, anyone can check out classical music or an educational video in addition to books.

5. Talk to your children's teachers. Encourage them to bring their best efforts into the classroom regardless of the political consequences. Then support them publicly, and particularly so in school controversies, when they ask your children to read important books. Go to school board and parents association meetings when there are likely to be narrowminded people presenting biased, ignorant, and intolerant opinions and counter those opinions with your own based on rationality, extensive reading experience, and the highest American ideals. Don't let the irrational elements of your local society have their day unopposed in front of the school board.

If your children are in college, go visit with some of their professors the next time you are on campus. Universities are magnificent places. They are not hotbeds of leftist political unrest and un-American drivel being foisted off on nubile coeds and helplessly credulous handsome young men. Universities are places where people achieve their highest goals, learn how to run complex societies, lift themselves up intellectually, become mature, thinking, well-trained humans who eventually assume positions of leadership in their communities.

Universities also play football. I've never been able to figure out why successful college graduates in general view their alma mater as a place to watch an athletic event but not a place to sit down for a serious talk with the faculty members who teach their sons and daughters. Conversely, faculty members owe it to themselves and their profession to visit openly and willingly with any parent who comes to their office.

6. Write letters to the local newspaper in response to irrationality. Form a group of like-minded rational people committed to answer irrationality quickly, articulately, and forcefully in the public pulse columns in letters to politicians. Send copies of your correspondence to ultraconservative relatives.

7. Volunteer to work in a rest home, an art museum, a natural history museum, a library. Teach reading to people who are functional illiterates. Remember your high school Spanish? Want to have a firsthand experience with a wrenching time in our history? Get involved as a volunteer helping immigrants adjust to the United States.

8. Comment on the narrative structure of television and films. Extend the discussion to include war as a test of manhood and a generator of heroes. Engage children and friends in conversations about violence in the media. Why did that person kill another? Why were weapons used in the solution of that problem? These are the lead questions to follow any experience in which violence is passed off as entertainment. Build up as heroes the people who prevent violence, who prevent war, the skillful diplomats who engineer international compromises instead of lead great armies into battle in which thousands of mothers' children get their faces and hands and feet blown away.

   Resist the use of women as objects in entertainment. Bash the typical made-for-television movie in which a very attractive woman is in danger and some man comes to save her, or in which an equally attractive woman loses her child and some man helps her get it back. Those story lines are aimed directly at our deepest emotions, and they define our place in this society on the basis of those emotions instead of on the basis of rational and well-educated citizenship. Now talk about what the entertainment industry is telling us not about violence per se, but about problem solving and gender roles in general.

9. Do an individual act that helps combat racism. Start simply. Say hello to the next individual you meet who is not of your ethnic background. Don't look past that person. Ask him or her some meaningful, nonstereotypical question. Next time you have an opportunity to act in a bigoted way, don't; next time you have an opportunity to act in a way that demonstrates racial tolerance, understanding, harmony, do it. Then look for the chances.

I'm sure there are a dozen additional ways in which single individuals can act small while thinking big. Are these suggestions idealistic? Of course; all attempts by individuals to influence the world in which they live are founded in idealism. All of the world's great religions are founded in idealism, as are all political movements. Any list of highly influential people is a list of outspoken idealists who found some way to communicate with the broad world beyond their immediate environs. Aristotle, Linnaeus, Karl Marx, Ralph Nader, Rachel Carson, Charles Darwin, Sigmund Freud, Pablo Picasso were idealists. All of these individuals are just that—*individuals*—with a message to convey and a self-sustained means of conveying it. Their visions of how the world is and how it ought to be are the products of their individual minds. The times in which they lived may have contributed something to their thoughts, but in that respect they are little different from any of the other nearly six billion people alive today. Do we personally have the power, through our individual actions, to make this world a more livable place, a gentler, kinder, more rational, less violent place?

Yes.

Yes. We do.

FIFTEEN

WHAT TO TELL YOUR CHILDREN

HOT BUTTONS

Eventually, one way or another, everyone deals with both religion and sex, so children need to know that sex and religion are natural parts of the human experience. Children need to learn how to control both of these forces because if they don't, others will do it for them. Our children will also eventually have to deal with weapons, liars and cheats, success and failure, money, and a long list of other things, too. But I begin this chapter with religion and sex because when it comes to children, those are the two parental hot buttons. They are also the two subjects in which many parents fail miserably as teachers. This failure is probably a result of the deep cultural, if not outright biological, origins of our sexual and spiritual emotions. By the time a child reaches puberty, his or her hormones and neural mystic networks may have come to override most parental influence on sex and religion. Kids go to Sunday School long before they go out on a date, however, so I'll begin with religion.

SUNDAY SCHOOL, HEAVEN, AND HELL

Children need to know that religion is not inherently dangerous. In fact, religion can be an enormously enriching and wonderfully mysterious part of the human experience. Religion is something we have and do in addition to, perhaps because of, not instead of, being human. There might be a heaven; we all might be united in heaven; I admit that possibility. But the belief that we and our children and parents and all parents and grandparents and future descendants will be united in heaven for an eternal life is just that—a belief, albeit one that gives many humans comfort and hope. So the belief that everyone, including even an obnoxious in-law who's accepted Jesus as his/her personal savior and won't let you forget it, will be united in heaven is a useful belief. But, just like reincarnation, heaven is still only a belief.

Children need to be told that the belief in heaven is a fundamental element of Western Christianity, not a tool with which a silver-tongued evangelist can extract money from a believer and replace that money with guilt. Of course there are hoards of slicks who'll do both, and add a measure of subservience to boot, as a reward for unquestioning belief. These claims are especially true if a child is female. So it's okay for an innocent young child to believe in heaven, so long as everyone understands that no matter how real heaven is *for you personally*, it still is only a belief. A wonderful, enormously powerful, inspiring belief, admittedly, but still only a belief. And, it is true, that belief in heaven can generate a heavenly life on Earth.

Hell, on the other hand, is a different matter. Most serious theologians have discarded the idea of physical hell and a Satan incarnate. So it's not okay to believe you're going to hell for playing cards, drinking coffee, dancing, or having been born a human being. Nor is it okay to indoctrinate our children to believe these same things. Anyone who's listened to enough cable television preachers realizes that this last sentence is fairly blasphemous.

In its most literal interpretations, Christianity holds that every human being is born in sin and cannot be saved without accepting Jesus as his or her personal savior. The concept of being born in sin is a truly awesome weapon. In practice, in the hands of a person with the right body language, this idea (meme) is a source of staggering power over others. Most of the highly successful televangelists have such body language and use it with great effect. My personal, although admittedly rather cynical, view is that one of the things that drive people to become televangelists is the recognition of just how much power they can get through skillful use of the idea that we are all born in sin.

The heaven that exists in the minds of devout Christians, especially fundamentalist ones, does not have any Muslim extremists or Buddhist monks walking the golden streets. Taken literally and technically, such a heaven does not have any babies in it, either, unless those babies were baptized before they died of Sudden Infant Death syndrome, various congenital problems, AIDS, or violence. One of the truly deep Christian theological problems is that of heaven and who gets to live there for eternity. Theologians have argued that issue for centuries. One of the more interesting problems in modern social psychology is the use of heaven and hell ideas to direct the behaviors of those who believe in both. In my personal view, if there is a real heaven somewhere beyond the Milky Way, and if any of us get there, we are likely to be shocked to find that a God who has the power to build a known universe also has room for all kinds of people who may not have sent their checks to Pat Robertson or Jimmy Swaggart or cast knee-jerk votes for Jesse Helms.

The ultimate heaven shock, however, given a God with the power to build the known universe, is the distinct possibility of encountering saved beings from other solar systems and galaxies. I'm guessing the average kid might find this possibility exceedingly interesting. Any guess as to what they might look like? Angels, probably. We'll all look like angels—slim, beautiful, young, strong—forever. There are a lot of products advertised on television that make the same claims. Maybe angels are so alive because of our deep-seated wishes to look like them.

The major take-home message for children on the subject

of religion is this: Humans practice religion because they're humans. In an ideal world, humans are free to practice whatever religion they want to. But the world is not ideal. Religious practices are also deeply ingrained cultural phenomena, and some nations and cultures greatly restrict a child's freedom to practice certain religions. The United States of America is not one of these rather constrained societies, at least in the matter of religion, as of this writing. We, and our children, are generally free to practice whatever religion we want to, and our children need to be told that fact from the time they are old enough to understand it (I suggest age three as a starting point).

The best way to make the United States a constrained and hostile religious environment, however, is to try to force *a* religion on everyone else, especially on children. Children generally don't understand political abstractions and theories until they get to puberty. Age twelve is about the time it's okay to start telling children that if they are successful in forcing everyone to accept their religion, then their own religious freedom eventually will be restricted. If you've done your parental homework—read to your children, talked to them about serious and interesting subjects at least part of the time, taken them to museums, art galleries, and zoos as well as to church—then they might listen. Regardless of whether it seems that they are listening or not, here is my advice: Keep talking to them about serious subjects and seeming paradoxes; that's what makes children grow up to be interesting people instead of dullards who can breed but can't carry on a conversation.

BASIC BIOLOGY

Unfortunately, biology works against us in our attempts to make serious thinkers out of our children. That is, about the time children get old enough to appreciate social paradoxes, they also get interested in the opposite sex. There is nothing anyone can do to prevent this from happening. Interest in the opposite sex is a fact of human life, as well as a fact of life for virtually every other species on Earth, although when it comes to beetles, for example, *interest* may not be the most appropriate term. Nevertheless, the vast and overwhelming majority of all species on Earth have only two choices: reproduce or die out. Inevitably, if able, they reproduce. Unless you're an amoeba, reproduction means sex.

Statistically speaking, reproduction is one of the most truly common behaviors exhibited by animals, including us. Behavior leading to reproduction is also an ingrained part of every species' genetic repertoire. Our children have these instincts. We wouldn't have children if we didn't have these instincts. So children *are* going to get interested in the opposite sex. A small fraction of them will also get interested in the same sex, but that's a separate problem. Thus we have to tell our children something about sex. What should we tell them? Ahhh! That is a most difficult question!

I don't have the answer, and I'm not sure anyone else does, either, including people who claim to have all the answers, so I'll begin with some advice based more on learning theory than on moral codes. We may not be able to tell our children anything about sex that contradicts too strongly the sexual information they begin receiving from society as a whole almost as soon as they can focus their eyes and push a button on the TV remote. We can, however, *show* our children the most fundamental aspect of healthy sexual behavior, namely respect for the opposite sex.

A father who is at home a reasonable amount of time, reads good books, and treats his wife with great respect, deferring to her in some important matters, and visibly appreciating her thoughts, ideas, and needs, is a powerful teacher, although he's teaching by example. A father who leaves his wife and daughter at home while he takes his son to the ball game, takes his son hunting, plops down in front of the Thursday night fights on TV with his son, insists on his bowling night out with the boys, and talks about how good looking certain women are, all in front of a wife and daughter, also is teaching by example. As a corollary, a wife who behaves like a materialistic bitch when treated with respect, or a wife who puts up with a husband's pathological good-ole-boy childishness, is an equally powerful teacher by example.

I'm not sure what kind of behavior is available to single parents to allow them to serve as role models in their child(ren)'s education about sex. Putting up with a long parade of abusive boyfriends is obviously something not to do, for a variety of reasons, if one can avoid it. But regardless of the circumstances, showing respect for members of the opposite sex, and demanding that they return that respect, is the first step in teaching children to show respect for their future spouses. When I review all of the variety of parental circumstances, however, I see plenty of unfortunate and unhappy, stressful situations that are not necessarily eliminated just by having a member of the opposite sex around. Sex education for children of single parents struggling under enormous burdens may be one of the truly difficult social problems to resolve. But I still think that self and mutual respect are the first, and most important, aspects of sex education, indeed, *any* education. And I've seen too many single parents who've taught their children these attributes to believe that a spouse is an indispensable part of the process, regardless of what the ultraconservatives claim.

SAYING NO

The second thing children need to know is that sex causes babies and that there are many reasonably effective ways to avoid having babies. On the other hand, there are more ways to avoid having sex than there are to avoid having babies. Female children need to understand that they, and they alone, have the right to decide when, where, under what circumstances, and by whom they will become pregnant. At the same time, they need to be clearly educated on three matters: (1) how to minimize their chances of getting raped and assaulted, (2) how to prevent pregnancy, and (3) what having an unwanted baby does to baby, mother, and society. Included in the instruction on how to prevent pregnancy must be the skills to say no. I don't know exactly how they accomplish it, but I've seen too many young women succeed at saying no to believe for one moment that saying no is an impossible task. Just from watching hundreds of young women operate in fairly volatile circumstances, I've become convinced that there is an extraordinarily interesting book to be written on the myriad ways for a female to say no. This book will be a best-seller and make someone obscenely rich and uncomfortably famous.

Clearly, saying no is an option for sons as well as daughters. Intelligent parents nowadays will try to figure out ways to convey, to their children, the social skills necessary to say no to themselves and to others. This effort will be a constant uphill battle, especially if a parent is telling a child to say no but at the same time worshiping televised and magazine glamour, slurping up the tabloids, and so forth. I don't possess any secrets in this business. I only know that some people are successful at it and others are not, so one must conclude that there *are* techniques for surviving adolescence and young adulthood, given a reasonable opportunity. Most of the young people I encounter who *seem* to be controlling their hormonal drives adequately also appear to have a great deal of respect for themselves. Some of them are devout members of various denominations, others are atheists; the one thing they have in common is their self-respect and their comfort with their humanity.

It's always seemed curious to me how parents of the strict conservative type can demand that their children be chaste, yet condemn public school efforts to teach self-esteem as "New Age Religion." I'm guessing that self-esteem is the most powerful ally a young person has in his or her struggle to make sense of sexuality and its many manifestations. You'd think parents would want their children to have a large supply of it, especially since it costs virtually nothing (the right words and body language). It is a strange paradox that female children of fundamentalist families do, on the average, pursue less postsecondary education, get married earlier (average age nineteen), and have children earlier than do female children of more liberal and humanist families. In this case, the strict Christianity has not worked to the long-term benefit of either the individuals or the society to which they belong. Some, of course, would argue that point. I would counter with the argument that a nation with its nineteen-year-old women married and with children is not a particularly healthy nation. I've seen far too many brilliant nineteen-year-old women who need to be in positions of power solving society's problems than home barefoot and pregnant in the kitchen to ever believe that early marriage is, on the whole, desirable for modern America.

BABIES

Children are not likely to listen to anyone on the subject of sex and unwanted pregnancy if that person displays an inordinate amount of emotional response to every baby, and especially to the *idea* of babies whenever given the chance. Babies are social, financial, and emotional burdens that dictate a parent's activities more effectively than almost any other force. Statistically speaking, parents cannot keep a daughter from getting pregnant by telling her to abstain from sex or by telling her that it's a sin to engage in sexual activity before marriage. Nor can parents keep a son from impregnating someone by preaching abstinence and sin. We can better our chances of keeping unwanted pregnancies out of our lives, again statistically speaking, by educating children in all areas of life, treating them with respect, teaching them about birth control (or encourage them to listen to that subject carefully in "health" class at school), and avoiding baby worship.

Babies are truly magnificent and wonderful experiences that need to be born to parents who want, love, and can afford them. Idea-babies, including the ones put into a daughter's head by going ga-ga over the concept of baby, have a way of becoming real infants that need to be fed, clothed, changed, taken to the doctor, and educated. Although it may be an affront to your religious "convictions," I'll state right out that admiration of couples with large families is a mistake, unless you want your own children to start having large families as soon as they are able to do so. Instead, children need to be told about the consequences of overbreeding.

Birth control and socially responsible breeding are both prerequisites to survival beyond the millennium. Large families are not necessarily good for society, especially if the parents had all the education, money, and means to stop having babies after a reasonable number. Each newborn American is destined to spend far more than his or her fair share of the world's energy resources simply because of the luck of having been born American. Yes, I do honestly believe that the Catholic Church is way out of line on the matter of birth control. That policy values the fact of life over the quality of life for all humans, not just Catholics, but Muslims and Jews, too, because non-Muslims and non-Jews consume resources that Muslims and Jews depend on. In the long term, that policy is completely counter to any other concerns the Catholic Church may seem to express for underprivileged or developing nation citizens. In other words, official Catholic policy on birth control for humans is the same as it is on birth control for beetles, snails, hyenas, and ducks. That policy is this: *Breed until you run out of resources, then die.* Ultraconservative religious rightists are looking forward to this day and have coined the ultimate euphemism for it: Rapture.

Gimme a break.

ULTIMATE WEAPONS

Aside from the sex and religion hot buttons, children also need to be told that in general they have nothing to fear from art, music, literature, science, the facts, and people who are different. But they also need to learn that people, whether similar or different from themselves, are often quite capable of committing dangerous acts. That is, there is no necessary correlation between being different and being dangerous. Nor is there any necessary relationship between sameness and safety, a fact revealed daily in most newspapers.

It is especially important for male children to know that they have nothing to fear, and in fact plenty to gain, from art, music, and literature. Art, music, and literature provide a person with interesting things to talk about, new ways of viewing the world, communication skills, and the self-confidence that comes from knowing you are well educated. But most importantly, art, music, and literature give a person access to the ideas of the ages, the ideas that have driven human beings through all recorded history to perform various acts of kindness, as well as acts of violence. In fact, if there is anything at all to be learned from a study of art, music, and literature, it's that ideas are the most powerful weapons humanity has, and no one has a monopoly on them. Teachers of art, music, and literature take note: If you are not teaching the idea power of your subjects, then you are failing in your responsibilities.

Children need to be told that it's okay to read books. In fact, we have an obligation to read to our children when they are young, take them to the library when they get older, give them books for presents so they will understand that we value books, and talk to them about what they've read. These books don't all have to be banned, ultra-liberal sex education literature. Believe it or not, one of my most treasured childhood books was Elsie Egermeier's *Bible Story Book*, given to me on my seventh birthday. When I was seven, I read these tales with great interest. They seemed to speak of grand deeds done and lessons learned the hard way. I particularly enjoyed the violence and reprisal of the Old Testament.

Now, as an adult reading the Bible, I'm less enamored with the self-serving violence, reprisal, and judgment of these same stories but more appreciative of their symbolic and metaphorical power. A book has certain attributes that other forms of communication lack. A book demands that a reader use his or her imagination, take the time to digest the contents, and read passages over and over again if necessary. Children need to be told that it's okay to mark important passages in their own books. I recommend a hard, well-sharpened pencil instead of a ballpoint pen. They can make notes and comments in the margins, too. Most well-educated people I know do this with their own books (i.e., the ones they buy themselves).

Children need to be told that they have our support when confronting nonrational behavior on the part of their peers, teachers, or other individuals. Irrationality is dangerous to everyone, and children need to learn that as early as possible. It's never too early to start teaching children to distinguish between belief and the facts as revealed by original observation. Your child's science classes are the place where these skills are best taught, provided the teacher knows what he or she is doing. No matter how much you *believe* that sugar won't dissolve in water, the demonstration counters that belief. Irrationality is basically the substitution of belief for observation.

If I have any final advice about what to tell our children in the next few years, aside from my opening comments on sex and religion, it would be the methods for learning to distinguish belief from observed facts. Read widely, be eclectic, try to keep your mind open, and always, *always* try to distinguish between belief and reality. I honestly think that of all the things a child can learn that will help him or her through many difficult times ahead, the techniques for distinguishing between belief and reality are the most valuable. I'm not claiming that reality is superior to belief, or vice versa. What I am saying is that the two are not necessarily connected regardless of how much we try to connect them, regardless of how much we try to force our children to merge belief and reality. Learning to distinguish between the two is the ultimate, and most basic, task of growing up.

And, our children will grow up, with or without our efforts to help them survive past midnight, December 31, 1999.

SIXTEEN

WHAT TO TELL YOURSELF

Reverend Martin Niemoeller, a German Lutheran pastor, was arrested in 1938 and sentenced to Dachau. He was liberated in 1945. Niemoeller is credited with the following statement:

> In Germany they came first for the Communists, and I didn't speak up because I wasn't a Communist. Then they came for the Jews, and I didn't speak up because I wasn't a Jew. Then they came for the trade unionists, and I didn't speak up because I wasn't a trade unionist. Then they came for the Catholics, and I didn't speak up because I was a Protestant. Then they came for me and by that time no one was left to speak up.

Niemoeller's statement is a guide, an inspiration, and a warning for individuals who find themselves in an increasingly irrational society. It tells of the inevitable expansion of tyranny that accompanies human attempts to impose uniform values, standards of behavior, and beliefs on societies, especially when that attempt is led by an egotistical, fragile ego. In a modern American context, one might say "In the United States, when the fundamentalists attacked the evolutionists, I didn't stand up because I wasn't a biology teacher," or "when the morality police closed the art museum, I didn't stand up because I never understood Abstract Expressionism." Or, on a more ominous note, "when we passed a city ordinance giving us permission to discriminate against homosexuals, I didn't write a letter to the editor because I didn't want people to think I was a homosexual." The principle is the same as it was in the Nazi Germany that Martin Niemoeller remembered.

Not everyone understands Abstract Expressionism, most (including me) find Darwin's books long and boring, and few of us, if any, really know what to think about homosexuality. What does it matter whether we resist the tyrants or not? It matters because tyranny takes a multitude of forms and knows no limits. The historical record is filled with examples, both great and small, of good intentions gone awry, utopias turned into hellish nightmares, cures worse than the afflictions, and "leaders" who lead seemingly happy, willing, intelligent people into calamitous circumstances. In all these cases, the human spirit is generally the loser.

If there was ever a phenomenon that possesses all the attributes of a classical, medieval, Christian Devil, it is the tyranny of the right. This Devil inhabits the bodies and minds of the truly evil as well as the well intentioned, spreads like wildfire through societies under stress and looking for relief, and catches everyone in its arms. It comes disguised as an immediate solution to perceived great problems. No one escaped Nazi Germany unscathed. The Auschwitz survivors now live with the knowledge that institutional memory of humanity's greatest horror is fading rapidly into oblivion, the process accelerated by a lunatic fringe that claims "it never happened." The tyranny of the right is intolerance, a pathological desire for homogeneity, fear of women, and an equally pathological illusion of correctness. The tyranny of the right consists of those conservative elements of the human psyche gone out of control.

The tyranny of the left is stupidity, especially in the management of human resources. However, the oppression of the left bears remarkable resemblance to the oppression of the right. Industry allowed to pollute, dissidence silenced, citizenry fed the sanctioned line, artists scorned unless they toed that sanctioned line—we remember these all too familiar events from Stalinist Russia. Yet these same characteristics are espoused today by the ultraconservative American right that would return us to the good old days of unregulated industry, a Bible and a prayer in every classroom, and art galleries with an excess of Hudson River landscapes on the walls.

But whereas the tyranny of the right is driven by a lust for power, that of the left is driven by insecurity and stupidity, mainly stupidity. No nation thrives unless its human potential is unlocked, allowed to flower in an intellectually fertile environment. The tyrannical right hates such flowers; the tyrannical left thinks the flowers can be cultivated. But at the extremes, the oppression of left and right come to resemble one another as if they were twins from the same womb. And, in a sense, they are. Political extremes, no matter how noble the ultimate goals, are a product of people who are afraid of their own humanity and who are working hard to strip others of theirs.

How is Satan to be kept at bay? Education, tolerance, and self-respect are the only truly effective weapons against the Devil tyranny. Of these, tolerance is the most crucial. But be leery of those who are quick to apply the "Liberal!" label in a disparaging way. Quite often their use of the word hides bigotry, hatred, insecurity, small-mindedness. When I say "tolerance" I'm not speaking here of all the current hot buttons so easily punched by the various sides in a political discourse: teenage violence and pregnancy, early release of convicted felons, massive government giveaways, special legal privileges for any particular group whether it be presidential advisers or gays and lesbians.

No, my "tolerance" is much more basic than "liberal." We must tolerate the finest, and often most humanist, aspects of our American culture. The free press is one of those finest features.

The freedom to practice a religion of choice is another. The exciting multicolored mixture of immigrant cultures is still another. So is free access to raw information, as is the freedom to contribute to the mass of raw information. I'm speaking here of freedom from censorship of all kinds. The freedom to meet in your home, or in a public place, and discuss virtually any topic from local property taxes to the voting record of your representative and senator is an enormous privilege, a humanist privilege. And any adult's freedom to engage in a private consensual sexual act with another adult is, regardless of what you think about it, as important as your right to protest your taxes and bear arms.

We've come to the point where we must tell ourselves: I cannot have my freedoms without defending the rights of others to have theirs; I cannot have my relatively dignified life on Earth without working to ensure that others have theirs. That relatively dignified life does not include the book of Revelation brought to fruition through human efforts of people convinced they're doing God's work, convinced they will be lifted to heaven when they've precipitated a nuclear exchange between Jews and Arabs, and equally convinced that everyone they hate will be consumed in the conflagration and have their souls banished to eternal hell.

It is time to admit that the rapturous utopian ideal, regardless of its basis—Christianity included—is the most seductive of grand delusions. From the Spanish Inquisition to Hitler's Germany it has brought us most of the truly miserable human conditions, the massive mistakes made in the name of adoration, the monumental botches originally conceived as final cures. In the closing years of the 20th century, the End Times theology of the fundamentalist Christians falls into the same category as those other tragic movements from the pages of history. Armageddon might come on its own in accordance with a biblical prophecy. A massive misery perceived as Armageddon will come if humans work hard to make it happen. In that event, the human-caused rapture will bear only superficial resemblance to the supposed God-caused Rapture (that is, if you use your imagination and metaphorical powers to interpret the results). In the end, the Grand Final Battle Between Good and Evil will look just like one more Typical Monumental Botch by Humans Convinced They're Operating Under Divine Edict.

Suppression of others' rights to make their statements, to show us their views, to argue our government's decisions, eventually leads to the suppression of our own. A world without offensive art is a world ripe for tyranny. A world without Muslims, Buddhists, atheists, controversial books, evolutionists, avant-garde filmmakers, left- and right-wing columnists, citizen action groups, religious fundamentalists, outrageous professors, crusading newspaper editors, prying reporters, well-stocked libraries, and an agnostic intelligentsia is an un-American world. A world in which the brightest, best-educated, and most successful people hide, stand back in the shadows while those in power march forward with their utopian dreams—the ethnic cleansing, the censorship in the name of morality, the self-delusion of creationists—is a deteriorating and soon to be dangerous world.

So what should we tell ourselves in order to survive past midnight, December 31, 1999? Ask questions. We learn, and grow, by asking questions and listening for answers, even when the questions are directed inward. The greatest minds in the world are those with the best questions. One of the significant problems in this world is that we seem to demand leaders who do more telling than asking. We want answers instead of uncertainty. But as soon as we stop asking questions, we stop learning. So as a result of our demands for answers we get leaders who are cases of arrested intellectual development. We don't have to have incompetents in high office, but choose them because we're afraid of people who ask questions and enamored of people who spout out answers regardless of whether these answers are right or wrong.

Run for office? Sure. Why not? Especially if you have the time, the right words and ideas, and can raise the money. On the other hand, I've seen common citizens, with absolutely no established power base and very little money, use their letter-writing skills, their telephone contacts, and their words to make a major, and positive, difference in the intellectual environments of their local communities, simply by figuring out who to write to and what to say and what kinds of questions to ask.

Join the intellectual elite? Sure; why not? In fact, you're probably already a member and don't realize it. Dan Quayle, vice president of the United States under George Bush, made much political hay by bashing the so-called intellectual elite. The very word *elite* has an anti-American ring to it. We pride ourselves on being a classless society, which of course we are not, with a government system in which everyone pays his fair share of taxes and carries her fair share of the burdens borne by a great nation, which of course he and she don't.

Statistically speaking, however, Americans are elite because they live in the United States. College (or equivalently) educated American citizens who have never spent time in jail, have a decent job, a house, a car, a similarly educated spouse, access to reasonable health care, including birth control information and methods, are all members of an elite group. Furthermore, most of us are not in Bosnia, Haiti, Rwanda, Guatemala, Cambodia, Calcutta, or Russia. When politicians attack the intellectual elite, they're not attacking half a dozen ruthless nerds who successfully force you to attend pornographic films, thereby transforming an upright Christian person into a violent, amoral one-worlder gay evolutionist. No, instead they're attacking Mr. and Mrs. Responsible Citizen with 2.5 typical children, who don't necessarily agree with the politicians about which movies to go see and which sitcoms to watch in the privacy of their own homes.

Sadly, too, *intellectual* is often considered an un-American word. The United States has never thought of itself as an intellectual nation. Americans consider themselves doers, pioneers, *men* of action, winners of wars. The American today actually is an urban black teenager planning his own funeral, a family farmer testing his soil for moisture so he can decide whether to pay for irrigation water, a teacher telling a middle-school student to take Spanish and learn to speak it well, a homosexual friend beaten up by some guys who waited in the parking lot outside a bar—just because his genes gave him a certain chemical makeup. It is time for Americans to grow up, read serious books, recognize the global forces that carry them along whether they are willing or not. Our soldiers and demagogues have had their say; it's time to listen to our philosophers, the people who understand how dumb ideas drive populations to destruction.

The most important thing to tell ourselves, however, is that just like every other person on this planet, we were born human. By virtue of that fact, we have all the brains, powers, hopes, frustrations, disappointments, delusions, creativity, analytical powers, successes, opportunities, and responsibilities of every other human who has ever been born and who ever will be born. That is, we have the potential for exhibiting both the best and the worst that humanity has to offer. I'm speaking statistically, of course, but because of the fundamental nature of humanity, each of us has every reason to believe any person can change the world into a better, safer, more rational place through individual actions.

In essence, the maintenance of a healthy society is in part an individual's responsibility. When a person denies, or declines to accept, that responsibility, then societies often degenerate into places where we see the worst side of our humanity, instead of the best. In Niemoeller's lament, he didn't stand up to the Nazis when they came for the Catholics because he wasn't a Catholic; in the end there was no one left to stand up for him. In a modern context, if well-educated, rational, and objective humans do not stand up to the forces of irrationality and mysticism, they will suffer the same fate.

It's a grand delusion that God is ready to return and cleanse the Earth. The End Times are not here just because the calendar finally turned to the year 2000. If the End Times are truly here, it's because we have brought them on ourselves by turning to the worst, instead of the best, that humanity has to offer itself. The worst is hatred, utopianism, intolerance, ignorance, and our ability to suspend the rules of physical reality in order to be part of a mythical heavenly kingdom. The best is rational and objective thought, an appreciation for nature and diversity, patience and tolerance, education, and freedom. In other words, it's long past time for us to act like human beings, exhibiting the finest of our evolved traits, instead of hanging on to the mysticism and self-delusions that are the luxuries of primeval societies.

APPENDIX: SUGGESTED READING

The following list of books is not intended to be definitive, nor to convince anyone that the views expressed in *Millennium* are correct. They will, however, test a reader's objectivity. You may have a similar list compiled from experience; if so, then feel free to share it with your friends. A few of the following books have influenced me very strongly; others are included simply as illustrations of particular ways of thinking. In some cases they tell the stories of people caught in the tides of history (e.g., the books by Freeman Dyson and about John von Neumann, Charles Darwin, and John Paul Vann). In other cases, they tell about the intellectual conflict between cultures (e.g., Tuchman's *Stilwell*). They deal with the mental mystique of high technology—Mailer's *Of a Fire on the Moon*, selected because the manned moonshots were our finest modern hour of exploration, an hour we've since abandoned. Reisner's *Cadillac Desert* tells us more about our relationships with the natural world than any other book I have read. Randy Shilts's *And the Band Played On* is a stunning and remarkable study of the relationships between culture, science, and medicine that, regardless of the subject matter (AIDS), is a warning of the costs of ignorance and bigotry.

Some of the titles deal directly with religion, especially apocalyptic themes. Too much has been written about eschatology to ever provide a summary, review, or evaluation of all this work. But the writing of *Millennium* required study of apocalyptic themes and the material suggested on the following pages is an introduction to the easily available literature on the subject.

SERIOUS AND SEMISERIOUS READING

Asimov, I. *Asimov's Guide to the Bible: Two Volumes in One—The Old and New Testaments.* Avenel, N. J.: Wings Books, 1981. 1295 pp.

Bates, Stephen. *Battleground: One Mother's Crusade, the Religious Right, and the Struggle for Control of Our Classrooms.* New York: Simon and Schuster, 1993. 365 pp.

Bedau, H. A. *Death Is Different.* Boston: Northeastern University Press, 1987. 307 pp.

Brzezinski, Z. *Out of Control: Global Turmoil on the Eve of the Twenty-first Century.* New York: Charles Scribner's Sons, 1993. 240 pp.

Carey, A. *The United States of Incompetence.* Boston: Houghton Mifflin, 1991. 203 pp.

Currie, E. *Confronting Crime: An American Challenge.* New York: Pantheon, 1985. 326 pp.

Curtis, L. A., ed. *American Violence and Public Policy: An Update of the National Commission on the Causes and Prevention of Violence.* New Haven: Yale University Press, 1985. 263 pp.

Desmond, A., and J. Moore. *Darwin.* New York: Warner, 1991. 808 pp.

Durant, W., and A. Durant. *The Lessons of History.* New York: Simon and Schuster, 1968. 117 pp.

Dyson, F. *Disturbing the Universe.* New York: Harper and Row, 1979. 283 pp.

———. *Weapons and Hope.* New York: Harper and Row, 1984. 340 pp.

———. *Infinite in All Directions: An Exploration of Knowledge and Belief.* New York: Harper and Row, 1988. 321 pp.

Ellul, J. *Apocalypse.* New York: Seabury Press, 1977. 283 pp.

Farb, P. *Man's Rise to Civilization as Shown by the Indians of North America from Primeval Times to the Coming of the Industrial State.* New York: E. P. Dutton, 1968. 332 pp.

————.*Word Play: What Happens When People Talk.* New York: Alfred A. Knopf, 1974. 350 pp.

Ford, D. F. *Three Mile Island: Thirty Minutes to Meltdown.* New York: Viking, 1982. 271 pp.

Fox, R. L. *The Unauthorized Version: Truth and Fiction in the Bible.* New York: Alfred A. Knopf, 1992. 478 pp.

Friedländer, S. *Reflections on Nazism: An Essay on Kitsch and Death.* New York: Harper and Row, 1984. 141 pp.

Fussell, P. *Wartime: Understanding and Behavior in the Second World War.* New York: Oxford University Press, 1989. 330 pp.

Halberstam, D. *The Reckoning.* New York: Morrow, 1986. 752 pp.

Halsell, G. *Prophecy and Politics: Militant Evangelists on the Road to Nuclear War.* Westport, Conn.: Lawrence Hill, 1986. 210 pp.

Heins, M. *Sex, Sin, and Blasphemy: A Guide to America's Censorship Wars.* New York: New Press, 1993. 210 pp.

Hesburgh, T. M. *The Humane Imperative: A Challenge for the Year 2000.* New Haven: Yale University Press, 1974. 115 pp.

Himmelfarb, M. *Tours of Hell: An Apocalyptic Form in Jewish and Christian Literature.* Philadelphia: University of Pennsylvania Press, 1983. 198 pp.

Hughes, R. *The Fatal Shore: A History of the Transportation of Convicts to Australia, 1787–1868.* London: Collins Harvill, 1987. 688 pp.

Koestler, A. *The Case of the Midwife Toad.* London: Hutchinson, 1971. 187 pp.

Kuhn, T. *The Structure of Scientific Revolutions.* Chicago: University of Chicago Press, 1970. 210 pp.

Kurtz, Paul. *In Defense of Secular Humanism.* New York: Prometheus, 1983. 273 pp.

LeShan, L., and H. Margenau. *Einstein's Space and Van Gogh's Sky: Physical Reality and Beyond.* New York: Macmillan, 1982. 268 pp.

LeShan, L. *The Psychology of War: Comprehending Its Mystique and Its Madness.* Chicago: Noble Press, 1992. 163 pp.

Lifton, R. J. *The Future of Immortality and Other Essays for a Nuclear Age.* New York: Basic, 1987. 305 pp.

McPhee, J. *Basin and Range.* New York: Farrar, Straus & Giroux, 1980. 216 pp.

————. *In Suspect Terrain.* New York: Farrar, Straus & Giroux, 1982. 210 pp.

————. *Rising from the Plains*. New York: Farrar, Straus & Giroux, 1986. 214 pp.

————. *Assembling California*. Farrar, Straus & Giroux, 1993. 304 pp.

Mailer, N. *Of a Fire on the Moon*. Boston: Little, Brown, 1970. 472 pp.

Marples, D. R. *The Social Impact of the Chernobyl Disaster*. New York: St. Martin's Press, 1988. 313 pp.

Mayr, E. *The Growth of Biological Thought*. Cambridge, Mass.: Harvard University Press, 1982. 974 pp.

Mayr, E. *Toward a New Philosophy of Biology: Observations of an Evolutionist*. Cambridge, Mass.: Harvard University Press, 1988. 564 pp.

Montagu, A. and F. Matson. *The Dehumanization of Man*. New York: McGraw-Hill, 1983. 246 pp.

Mostert, N. *Supership*. New York: Warner, 1976. 382 pp.

Nader, R. *Unsafe at Any Speed*. New York: Grossman, 1972. 153 pp.

Neo-Fundamentalism: The Humanist Response. Presented by the Academy of Humanism. Buffalo, N.Y.: Prometheus, 1988.

Newell, N. D. *Creation and Evolution: Myth or Reality?* New York: Columbia University Press, 1982. 199 pp.

Novik, S. *The Electric War: The Fight over Nuclear Power*. San Francisco: Sierra Club Books, 1976. 376 pp.

Numbers, P. L. *The Creationists*. New York: Alfred A. Knopf, 1992. 458 pp.

Paz, O. *The Labyrinth of Solitude*. New York: Grove Press, 1985. 398 pp.

Peters, T. *Futures: Human and Divine*. Atlanta: John Knox Press, 1978. 192 pp.

Poundstone, W. *Prisoner's Dilemma*. New York: Doubleday, 1992. 294 pp.

Radest, H. B. *The Devil and Secular Humanism: Children of the Enlightenment*. New York: Praeger, 1990. 170 pp.

Reisner, M. *Cadillac Desert*. New York: Viking, 1986. 582 pp.

Russell, J. B. *Mephistopheles: The Devil in the Modern World*. Ithaca: Cornell University Press, 1986. 333 pp.

Schwartz, J. *The Creative Moment: How Science Made Itself Alien to Modern Culture*. New York: HarperCollins, 1992. 252 pp.

Sheehan, N. *A Bright Shining Lie: John Paul Vann and America in Vietnam*. New York: Random House, 1988. 861 pp.

Shilts, R. *And the Band Played On*. New York: St. Martin's Press, 1987. 646 pp.

Smith, H. *Essays on World Religion*. Edited by M. D. Bryant. New York: Paragon House, 1992. 290 pp.

Thomas, L. *Lives of a Cell*. New York: Viking Press, 1974. 153 pp.

Tuchman, B. *Stilwell and the American Experience in China, 1911–45*. New York: Macmillan, 1970. 621 pp.

Weatherford, J. *Savages and Civilization: Who Will Survive?* New York: Crown, 1994. 310 pp.

Wilson, E. O. *On Human Nature*. Cambridge, Mass.: Harvard University Press, 1978. 260 pp.

Wolfson, R. *Nuclear Choices: A Citizen's Guide to Nuclear Technology*. Cambridge, Mass.: MIT Press, 1991. 467 pp.

Wyatt, C. R. *Paper Soldiers: The American Press and the Vietnam War*. New York: W. W. Norton, 1993. 272 pp.

A Couple of Polemical Low-Quality Books That Can Be Read to Put the Rest of the Bibliography into Its Proper Perspective

Bennett, William J. *The Devaluing of America: The Fight for Our Culture and Our Children*. New York: Simon and Schuster, 1992. 271 pp.

Silber, J. *Straight Shooting: What's Wrong with America and How to Fix It*. New York: Harper and Row, 1974. 336 pp.

Samples of Some Truly Wacko Stuff

Hartman, J. *What Will Heaven Be Like?* Dunedin, Fla.: Lamplight Publications, 1991. 137 pp., plus twenty pages of advertisements for other Hartman books and tapes.

Jeffrey, G. R. *Armageddon: Appointment with Destiny*. New York: Bantam, 1988. 235 pp., plus appendixes.

Lindsey, H. *The Late Great Planet Earth*. Grand Rapids, Mich.: Zondervan Publishing, 1970. 192 pp.

Reik, T. *Myth and Guilt: The Crime and Punishment of Mankind*. New York: George Braziller, 1957. 432 pp.

INDEX

nonreligious, and apes,
118–19
and Ten Commandments,
120–22
and Tree of Knowledge,
97–98
Multiculturalism, 93
Multiple reality domains,
131
Murder, 120
Music, 69, 102, 155, 162
Muslims, 90
Myth and Guilt (Reik), 48
Mythical reality, and war,
131

Nader, Ralph, 144
Nagasaki, 103
Nakedness, 100–101
Narcotics, 88
National Advisory Commission
on Civil Disorders (1967),
111
National Commission on the
Causes and Prevention of
Violence (1968), 111
National Endowment for the
Arts, 36
Natural history museums,
139–40, 143
Natural law, 66
Natural resources, 141
Nazi Germany, 6–7, 124, 158,
159, 161
Nevelson, Louise, 39
New English Bible (Cambridge
University Press), 28–29
Newspapers, 67–68, 143

New World Order, 130
New Yorker, 29, 142
Niemoeller, Rev. Martin, 158,
164
Nixon, Richard, 9
Noah and the Flood story,
48–50
Nonfiction books, 141
Nonhuman species, 62
Nuclear weapons, 103–4

Oil
and Arabs, 91
need for, 127, 128
running out of, 18, 19
Old Testament, 29, 90
On Human Nature (Wilson), 80,
90, 109
Opportunity, 92, 114
Organized religion
corporate behavior of,
64
and domination of women,
99
and first millennium,
13–14
and human misery, 4
and sex, 72–75
and technology, 47
Original sin, 72, 147–48
Origin of life, 61–62
Origin of Species (Darwin),
60
"Other"
and homophobia, 80–82
and racism, 93–94
Otto I, Emperor of Germany,
14